THE LOGICAL THINKING PROCESS

An Executive Summary

by

H. WILLIAM DETTMER

DISCLAIMER

Several illustrations in this book were obtained from the Internet, and no source or attribution was associated with them. Every effort was made to determine the originator and obtain permission, without success. The author is willing to provide compensation to the artists who created the illustrations in Figures 1.1, 1.3, and 2.4. Contact the author at gsi@goalsys.com.

Cover designed and produced by
Lion's Den Studio
East Brunswick, New Jersey
(732) 828-8550

"The Logical Thinking Process – An Executive Summary" by H. William Dettmer. ISBN 978-1-947532-49-6.

Published 2018 by Virtualbookworm.com Publishing Inc., P.O. Box 9949, College Station, TX 77842, US. ©2018, H. William Dettmer.

INTRODUCTION

THERE IS A SERIOUS LACK OF CRITICAL THINKING in the world to-day. People everywhere are bombarded with information from the Internet, magazines, newspapers, television, social media, and e-mail. Some of this information is "signal." Most of it is "noise." Most people accept at face value the validity (or veraci-ty) of the interpretation those reporting this information give us. In other words, we often put our faith — for plans, decisions, and actions — in the hands of those who deliver and interpret the in-formation we receive. That's dangerous.

Critical thinking helps us separate the signal from the noise. It helps us avoid the pitfalls inherent in taking what we hear and see at face value.

Even so, once that signal is separated from noise, we're faced with the challenge of deciding what to do about what we know — both the resident historical knowledge and any new in-formation we may have sifted from the mass input that sweeps over us each day. We find ourselves trying to answer some basic questions:

How does this information affect me?

How can I evaluate its validity?

What ramifications does it have for my life and work?

What should I do with this information?

In isolation, these seem like simple enough questions. But let's put them into a personal context. Here's the situation: The persistent, ever-growing problem of sovereign debt (both inter-national and domestic) finally reaches a head: the house of cards that is the international financial system is on the verge of be-ginning a tsunami-like collapse. Let's call this a *problem statement.*

It hasn't happened (yet), but a lot of people in many countries are increasingly concerned about it.

Now, in light of this problem statement, let's revisit those four questions above. Not so easy to answer, are they? But are they *unanswerable?* I submit that they're not. What makes them so difficult (and intimidating) to try to answer is the lack of an effective way to structure and evaluate the information so as to give us a clearer picture of the situation, where we stand in it, and what our options for the future are.

In the late 1980s, Eliyahu M. Goldratt, an Israeli physicist, conceived a set of logical tools he referred to as *the thinking processes.* His aim was to use them to define complicated real-world situations in easy-to-read and absorb cause-and-effect diagrams that would reveal the true underlying causes of complex system problems—leverage points—and suggest ways to resolve them. In other words, he wanted to find those few changes (decisions or actions) that could produce the broadest, deepest positive impact on the systems we live in and work with every day.

Over the course of the next thirty years, these thinking processes have matured and been refined into what today is known as the *Logical Thinking Process* (LTP). There are books about this LTP (see the bibliography at the end of this book). These books go into great detail on the construction and use of the logical tools of the LTP. This book is more of an overview. It's intended to acquaint leaders—executives, managers, elected officials, and even community thought leaders—with the LTP: what it is, generally how it works, and how leaders might use it to help them think critically about the problems and issues they face. If you're a leader (or consider yourself one), let this book help you decide whether it's worth your time to investigate the LTP more deeply.

H. WILLIAM DETTMER

Port Angeles, Washington, USA

February 2018

Table of Contents

CHAPTER 1.

The Logical Thinking Process: An Effective Solution

It is a simple thing to make things complex, but a complex task to make them simple.

— Meyer's Law [1]

THOUGH YOU MAY BE UNFAMILIAR with the Logical Thinking Process (LTP), it's not especially new. In various forms, it's been around for 25 years. During that time it has definitely "morphed." [2] The evolution has come through practical use and deliberate refinement. Because its name includes the word *logical*, it's important to understand that there are rational reasons why we follow the approach and procedures that we do. This chapter will explain both the approach and the overall steps in the process.

"Soup to Nuts"

The LTP represents a promising solution to the challenge of complex system problems—the kind where many different factors may contribute to the visible indications of a problem. Moreover, the chain of cause and effect between our system deficiencies and their underlying causes is often not obvious. Sometimes we're even fooled by reality and "conventional thinking" into assuming that something is the root cause of our problem, when in fact it isn't.

---

[1] Dettmer. *He Said, She Said*, p.114

[2] Much as software companies often introduce a "not quite ready for prime time" product to the market, expecting to refine it later, Goldratt introduced "the thinking processes" to the public in the early 1990s, without much supporting documentation or "how and why" explanation. Consequently, the methodology has evolved over time. The Logical Thinking Process is the latest and most precise evolution of the method.

Because our systems are complex, it might be difficult even to define our problems, much less to come up with workable solutions to them. *The LTP is designed to start with an ill-defined problem and take us all the way through to a fully implemented solution —* one that is "bullet-proofed" to the extent that it's possible to do so.

Change (That dreaded word!)

Figure 1.1 - Change
"There is a rumor going around that change is coming. I want YOU to make sure that it doesn't get into THIS building!"

Implicit in the idea of solving problems is the concept of *change*. An old saying goes, "If you always do what you've always done, you'll always get what you've always gotten." This statement implies an underlying structure of cause and effect. If we're not happy with the results we're seeing, we're compelled to do something different to change those results... unless we're willing to wait and depend on fate to make things better. On the other hand, if we're completely satisfied with the results we're

getting, we had better understand *why* what we're currently doing produces those results. Otherwise, when the situation
changes—as it inevitably will—we won't recognize that what
we've always done is no longer adequate for our needs. Addi-
tionally, even if we recognize the need to change *before* it becomes critical, we might not understand our system well enough
to know what we should do differently.

Anybody's "improvement" is somebody's change. And
change is not a pleasant prospect for everybody. That's a psychological issue, not a technical one. The trick is to make changing our systems as painless as possible. So, consider the LTP to
be your trusted "navigational aid." It can tell you why what
you're doing now is the right thing to do (if, in fact, it is). But
more important, it can tell you why your current practices are
failing and help you navigate through the change, whether mi-
nor or major, to correct your system's course so than you can
safely reach your chosen destination... in other words, your
goal.

The LTP answers four crucial questions any leader or executive needs to know:

1. *Why* should I change what we're doing?
2. *What* should I change?
3. *What and how* should we do things differently? (This is
   usually expressed as "what to change *to*?")
4. *How* can I best make that change happen?

You'll notice my liberal use, above, of the personal pronoun
"I." That's deliberate. The reason is that ultimately, "the buck
stops here." [3] Like the captain of a ship, leaders are responsible
for what happens to their organizations—whether good *or* bad.

In early days of aviation, pilots flew open-cockpit biplanes
by the seat of their pants. In other words, through intuition and

---

[3] Former U.S. President Harry S Truman famously kept a placard on his desk in
the White House that read "The buck stops here," meaning that there was no
higher authority (or responsibility). This is true of any executive, though many
sometimes choose to try to evade that responsibility.

feel, not complicated analysis. When such planes had but one engine and but a few instruments, this method worked adequately... most of the time. But when airplanes became as complicated as the ones we have today, considerably more structure, both procedural and regulatory, was needed to maximize success, especially when things started going sour. The same is true of our organizational systems today. And the LTP can provide the "pilot" of the organization the logical structure he or she needs to make good decisions... and to ensure that subordinates do, too.

The Logical Thinking Process Roadmap

The LTP is comprised of five separate logic trees. Each one has a specific purpose.

- Goal Tree – Where do we *want* to be?
- Problem (Current Reality) Tree – Where *are* we, actually, and *why* is there a difference?
- Conflict Resolution Diagram (Evaporating Cloud) – What prevents us from curing the problem *now*, and *how* do we overcome it?
- Solution (Future Reality) Tree – What can we *expect* to happen if we apply a "fix" to the problem?
- Implementation (Prerequisite) Tree – How do we make the solution happen — that is, execute the solution?

While the original concept was for all of these logic trees to be used in sequence to solve a complex system problem, in reality it's possible that this might not be necessary. Consequently, each of the logic trees (tools) can also be pulled out and used individually, as the situation dictates.

The Goal Tree

Of these five trees, the central (and most critical) one is the Goal Tree. This is the tool that helps formulate precisely what our desired outcome is. In other words, what are we trying to achieve — our system's *goal*. Why is this the most crucial of all the trees? In the words of Mabel Newcomber, "It is more important to know where you're going than to get there quickly. Do not mistake activity for accomplishment." [4]

Consider the Goal Tree to be a navigation marker or benchmark. It provides the fixed, immutable point of reference for *all* the other tools. For that reason, our LTP roadmap looks more like a wheel with spokes, the Goal Tree lying at its hub. (**Figure 1.2**)

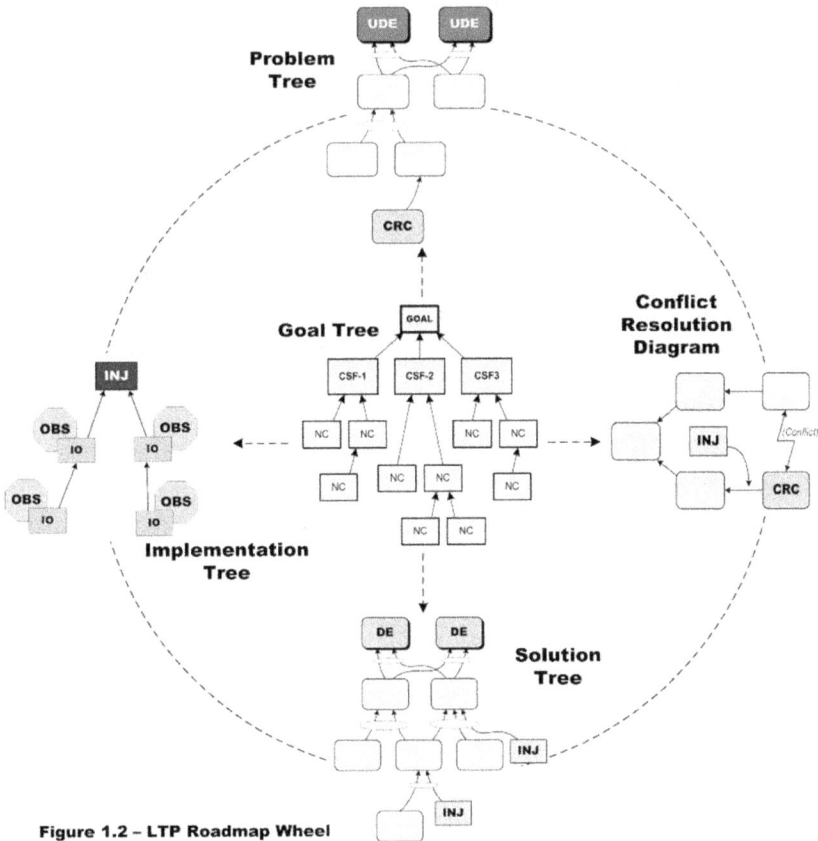

Figure 1.2 – LTP Roadmap Wheel

The Goal Tree is at the center of everything. That's because it establishes the ultimate destination of an organizational system: what its purpose is and what must be done to achieve it. Consequently, the elements of the Goal Tree provide a reliable *bench-*

---

[4] Dettmer. *He Said, She Said*, p.50.

mark for the definition of problems, the resolution of internal conflicts, strategizing for the future, and, of course, execution of plans, projects and changes.

What do I mean by a benchmark? In every phase of operations, it lets us feel comfortable with the answers to these questions:

- Are we on course toward our goal?
- Are we doing the things we *should* be doing to get there? If not, what's missing?
- Are we doing things that don't contribute to the early attainment of our goal? If so, what should we stop doing?
- How do we know when we've achieved our goal?

At each stage of our complex problem solving process, the Goal Tree provides reassurance that we're doing the *right* things—but not necessarily doing things *right*. That's the function of the logic trees on the perimeter of our wheel. In Chapter 3, you'll see a clearer picture of how the Goal Tree does this.

The Problem Tree[5]

It's been said that a well-defined problem is more than half solved. Why is this so? Because, especially in our complex world, it's not necessarily easy to know what the real cause of our disaffection with our situation might be. For example, consider a manufacturing company that experiences a large number of returned items that failed in the hands of the end user. The warranty costs associated with making the end user satisfied can add up quickly, creating a serious hit to the company's bottom line. But what is the actual cause of the failure? User abuse? Manufacturing defect? Defective raw materials? Design deficiency? Inadequate operating instructions?

Any of these might be the prime cause, or perhaps more than one contributes to the unfavorable end results. There is no short-

---

[5] The Problem Tree has been historically called a current reality tree, because it characterizes the cause and effect behind what is actually happening in the organization's situation now.

age of process improvement tools available through methodologies such as six sigma, total quality management, lean, etc.

But what if our problem is the *system itself?* The company as a whole isn't succeeding as expected. It might even be losing money. Or it may be outpaced by its competition. In such cases, the undesirable outcomes are obvious. The underlying causes might not be. And process improvement tools aren't much help. You can decide that the production process needs to be "leaned up." But what assurance do you have that this is really the problem? As the Emperor Nero did, you could be "fiddling while Rome burns." (**Figure 1.3**)

Figure 1.3 – Nero Fiddles While Rome Burns

An effective Problem Tree does two things for you. First, it identifies the real critical root causes of the adverse indications you see. And second, it provides the logical rigor that substantiates the proper root cause identification. In other words, it can give you the confidence that you're working on the *correct* issues. Chapter 4 will give you a better understanding about how this happens.

The Conflict Resolution Diagram[6]

Any organization experiences conflict at one time or another. It could be *internal* or *external*. It might be a dispute between the company and its customers, or perhaps between departments within the company, or even individuals. It could be overt or subtle (hidden). In any case, conflict is most insidious when it hinders or completely frustrates the company's progress toward the attainment of its goal.

One of the most common expressions of conflict in any organizational system is *resistance to change*. This resistance has its basis in human psychology and almost always results from people's concern for their own welfare, which they will usually worry about more than the welfare of the organization. As Niccolò Machiavelli observed:

> ...there is nothing more difficult to arrange, more doubtful of success, and more dangerous to carry through than initiating changes. The innovator makes enemies of all those who prospered under the old order, and only lukewarm support is forthcoming from those who would prosper under the new... Their support is lukewarm ... partly because men are generally incredulous, never really trusting new things unless they have tested them by experience.[7]

In other words, an organizational change—and organizations don't get better by staying the same— faces resistance from those whose "ox gets gored" by the change, but also those who fear an uncertain future.

The Conflict Resolution Diagram is the Logical Thinking Process's prescription for smoothing the path of change by anticipating and resolving potential (or real) conflicts before they can adversely affect the "new order of things." We'll see how this happens in Chapter 5.

---

[6] The Conflict Resolution Diagram was originally called an "evaporating cloud" by its creator, E.M. Goldratt. We prefer a name that more accurately describes, in a very few words, what the tool actually does.

[7] http://www.azquotes.com/author/9242-Niccolo_Machiavelli

The Solution Tree[8]

A well defined problem may be more than half solved, but there's still a huge leap forward to make: turning a great improvement idea into reality. As the American cowboy-philosopher, Will Rogers, once said, "Plans get you into things, but you have to work your own way out." [9] So many great ideas have collapsed for want of two crucial things: 1) Verification that the idea will actually work, and 2) Failure to successfully execute the change. The Solution Tree addresses the first of these two requirements.

Consider the implementation of a significant systemic change to be a project. Success requires three things (or, as the Goal Tree might indicate, critical success factors):

- Performance (the change has to do what it was intended to do)
- Schedule (it has to happen sometime in the reasonably near future), and
- Cost (it must not break the budget)

To ensure that our proposed organizational change succeeds, it would be a lot more reassuring to know, first and foremost, that it will achieve the results that we desire and do so without creating any new, insurmountable adverse outcomes. As Eric Sevareid once observed, "The chief cause of problems is solutions." [10] This is a shorthand way of saying that we tend to make things more difficult for ourselves in the future by not confirming that what we want to do will actually work and by failing to anticipate how our new idea could cause new, more, or worse problems than we already have.

The Solution Tree is the Logical Thinking Process's answer to "bullet-proofing" our new plans for the future. In Chapter 6, we'll see how that happens.

---

[8] The Solution Tree is also referred to as a "future reality tree," because it describes the cause and effect behind the new concept that we want to put into place, but which isn't there yet.

[9] Dettmer, *He Said, She Said*, p. 101.

[10] Ibid., p. 114.

The Implementation Tree[11]

The final step in instituting a change in organizational direction is execution. You may have this great new idea, but harking back to Will Rogers' words, above, "...you have to work your own way out." And, as some wise philosopher once said, "The devil is in the details." The Implementation Tree is the Logical Thinking Process's orderly way of defining and structuring those nagging details.

Now, as you can undoubtedly imagine, orchestrating a major system change involves accomplishing a lot of individual tasks. Many of these are quite straightforward: "Do *this* one thing, and you're done." For tasks like this, it's sufficient to take the project approach: define the task (performance), decide when it has to be completed (schedule), allocate the resources (cost) to get it done, and assign accountability for its completion to a specific person.

But in any significant organizational change, there will always be some important things to be done that are much more complicated than a simple task.

For example, consider a large international mining concern with 35 mine operations all around the world. A few years ago, the chairman and chief executive officer of this company decided that he needed a new, single information system that could integrate decision information worldwide, from each of the 35 separate mine operations. (Because most of these various mines had been acquired through purchase or corporate merger, the information systems were different.) Integrating information flow from 35 different sources into a standardized common format, understandable by anyone in the system, was a hugely complicated undertaking. In fact, it required five years to accomplish.

But the basis for managing this complex project was what the Implementation Tree provides: a clear definition of what must be done, in what order, what must be done in sequence, and

---

[11] The Implementation Tree is also referred to as a "prerequisite tree," because it structures all the discrete tasks that must be accomplished—the prerequisites—for successful execution of our changes.

what can be done in parallel. Chapter 7 will provide a clearer picture of how the Implementation Tree helps to do this.

Conclusion

As Machiavelli observed, undertaking change in any organization can be fraught with peril. Careers can be made by completing such changes successfully. Or destroyed by failing to do so. How much comfort would *you* derive from having a series of tools — the Logical Thinking Process — to help you maximize your odds of success the first time?

> *The hardest thing to learn in life is which bridge to cross and which bridge to burn.*
>
> — *David Russell* [12]

---

[12] Dettmer. *He Said, She Said*, p.66.

CHAPTER 2.

Strategic Direction: The Goal Tree

The beginning is the most important part of the work.

— Plato [13]

IT DOESN'T REALLY MATTER how simple or how complicated your system is. Leaders of all systems face the same challenge: *How to ensure the success of their system.* But how do we define "success?" Different people see the answer differently, but in the final analysis, success is the *achievement of the purpose for which the system was designed.* Which raises another question: *Who gets to define that purpose?*

Essentially, the answer is the owner of that system. Whatever the owner says is the system's purpose, that's what it is. The owner could be an individual, a family, a group of private investors, or perhaps the stockholders in a publicly traded company. But that's only for commercial businesses.

The system might be a government agency. Who's the owner in *that* case? In a government "of the people, by the people, and for the people," that would be the citizens of the city, state, or country that the governmental system is intended to serve.

A not-for-profit system, such as a charitable organization, would have a goal, too. But in this case it's a little different. There are no stockholders and no citizen-voters, per se, to qualify as owners. But there *is* a board of directors, who, much like the board of directors of a commercial company, are for all intents and purposes the system's owners.

---

[13] Dettmer. *He Said, She Said*, p.102

Mission, Vision and Values

Nearly everyone in the business and government world is familiar with the concept of mission, vision, and values statements. With the advent of total quality management in the 1980s, defining one's mission, vision, and values statements became "the thing to do," and organizations devoted no small amount of time to articulating these statements. Often, the senior executives and managers decamped to an "off-site" location, spending a weekend in isolation coming up with such statements.

The net result of such efforts was inevitably a "feel good" effect—"Okay, we've checked *that* box... now it's back to work." And in many cases the effort to come up with these statements produced nothing of lasting value, since the mission, vision, and values were often confined to frames on the wall of the reception room of the organization—and largely ignored!

It's a shame that these dedicated efforts to produce mission, vision, and values statements were, more often than not, wasted. If the leaders of the system knew what to do with them, these statements were a potentially valuable contributor to system success. I would even say that they could have provided the bedrock foundation for everything the organization subsequently did.

Why did this not happen? I submit that it's because the leaders failed to understand the connection between these three statements and the daily tasks and functions of the system. In other words, they failed to see a strategic connection between these higher level ends and the system's activities. That strategic connection is depicted in **Figure 2.1**.

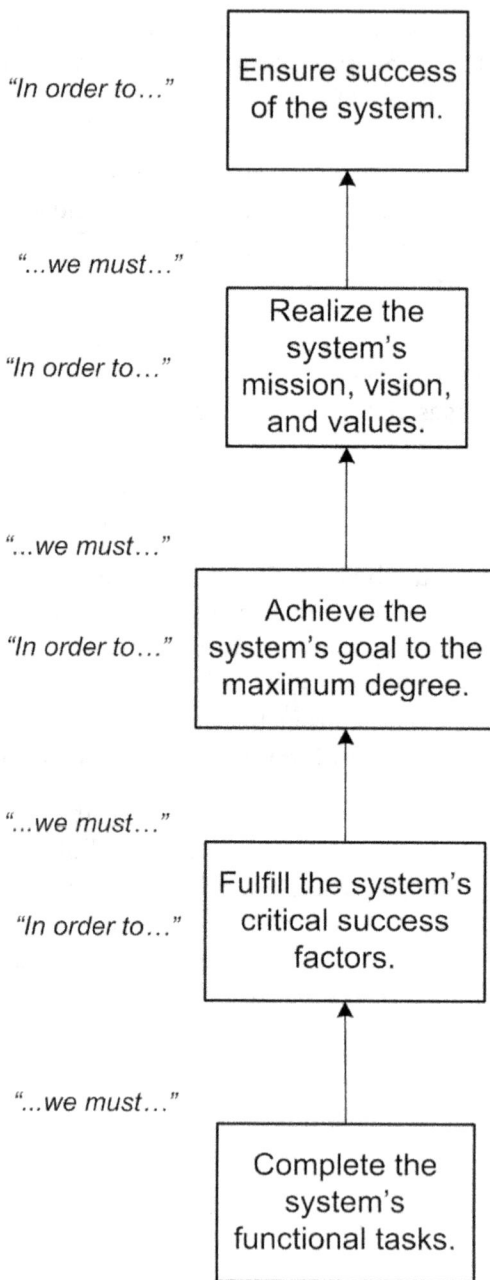

"*In order to...*"   Ensure success of the system.

"*...we must...*"

"*In order to...*"   Realize the system's mission, vision, and values.

"*...we must...*"

"*In order to...*"   Achieve the system's goal to the maximum degree.

"*...we must...*"

"*In order to...*"   Fulfill the system's critical success factors.

"*...we must...*"   Complete the system's functional tasks.

Figure 2.1 The Strategic Hierarchy

What many people fail to realize is that mission accomplishment and ultimate system success aren't stand-alone things. They exist in *a hierarchy of dependent actions* and achievements that are not always intuitively obvious. In order to be successful, a system must accomplish its mission, realize its vision of the future, and in doing so adhere to its stated values.

As you can see in Figure 2.1, a key requirement in doing this is achieving the stated goal of the system owners. But even that doesn't stand alone. Goal attainment requires the fulfillment of a limited set of critical success factors (CSF) that collectively define the goal. These CSF are indispensable components of goal attainment. But even these are *high-level terminal system outcomes —* requirements — and it's normally not clear how they're satisfied without drilling deeper into the system.

The CSF are fulfilled by discharging the daily tasks and responsibilities of the system at the working levels. These are the functional activities that deliver the component contributions to achieving the system's goal. In summary, all systemic functional activities are linked to the success of the system through a vertical hierarchy of successively higher outcomes, as shown in Figure 2.1.

So, even if we have an ultimate purpose — a mission — and a vision of what we want our future to look like, we lack a way to connect the day-to-day efforts and activities of the system to these higher level aspirations. Absent that clear connection, we risk replicating the experience of the Roman Emperor Nero (Figure 1.2): In other words, too much of our attention is devoted to things that don't matter... things that consume valuable resources (time, money and skill) yet don't contribute in any meaningful way to fulfilling the system's mission.

In fact, without a clear understanding of the vertical dependency between action and outcome, many of the formal activities that take place in most systems are akin to rearranging the deck chairs on the *RMS Titanic* after it stuck the iceberg.

The Missing Link: A Goal Tree

Let's assume you accept the necessity of a way to link the day-to-day activities of your system with its overall success — to confidently assure that everything happening within your system actually contributes to the greater good. How can one do that?

The Logical Thinking Process provides the answer in the form of a Goal Tree (GT). What, exactly, is a Goal Tree? In short, it's the lower part of that strategic system hierarchy — the bottom three components. (**Figure 2.2**)

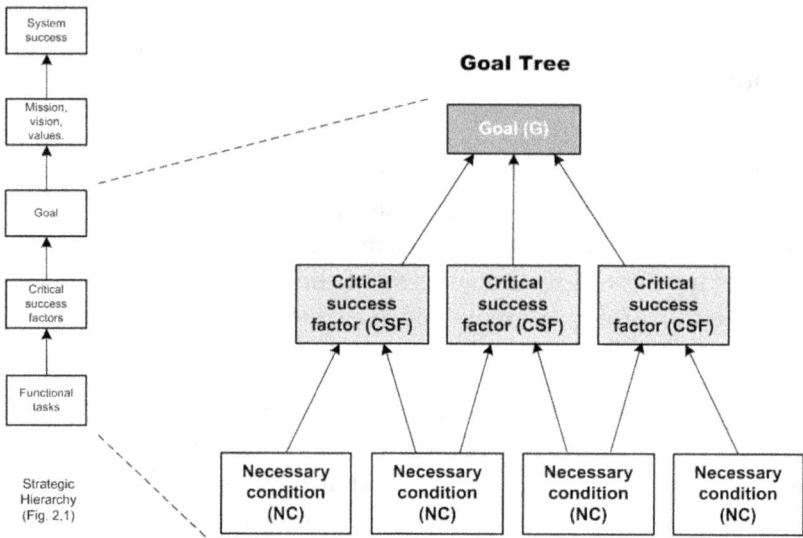

Figure 2.2 The Goal Tree

Notice that the fulfillment of the system's mission depends on achieving its goal. Achieving that goal contributes directly to mission accomplishment. But what is the difference between a goal and a mission? Opinions on the meanings of the two terms may differ, but in the interest of clarity let's begin with this distinction:

> *Mission: A high level purpose which survives indefinitely as long as the system exists.*

> *Goal: A long-term measurable outcome that, when achieved, clearly connotes mission accomplishment.*

Consider goal attainment to be *a visible indicator of mission accomplishment.*

Here are two examples, one for a commercial for-profit system and one for a not-for-profit system: An automobile manufacturer and a research fund-raising organization.

Toyota

Everyone knows of Toyota, one of the most successful automobile manufacturers in the world, renowned for quality and value for the price of their vehicles. Their mission might be to become the pre-eminent automobile company in the world ("We're number one!"). Their vision might be to produce cars of such high quality and value that all competitors aspire to equal them. And their values might include environmental, economic, and societal responsibility.

Their goal, however, might be to make as much money as they can while adhering to their values. But here's the rub: missions can change while goals remain the same. Conversely, goals can change while missions remain the same.

It has been reported[14] that Toyota has a hundred year strategic plan envisioning the day when automobile production might not be the majority of their business. Their leaders have anticipated that there will eventually be limits to the expansion of automobile sales worldwide. And they foresee that the great unfulfilled worldwide demand in the 21st century will be for high-quality, low-cost housing.

In that case, their mission might change. Instead of being the pre-eminent automobile producer, they would become the pre-eminent provider of affordable housing worldwide. Yet their goal — to make as much money as they can while doing so — would not change.

---

[14] Holley, David. "Toyota heads down a new road," Los Angeles Times, Business, Part D (March 16, 1997)

Mothers' March of Dimes

In the 1940s, the scourge of health in the industrialized world was polio myelitis, sometimes known as infantile paralysis, because it so often struck little children. Adults were not immune to it, however, and perhaps its most notable victim was US President Franklin D. Roosevelt.

In 1947, the Mother's March of Dimes (MMD) was organized with the goal to support the search for a cure for polio. MMD was very successful. By 1954, a vaccine for the prevention of polio was perfected. By 1960, it was widely dispensed, and by the late 1960s, polio was largely eradicated from the face of the earth... leaving a well-developed, mature fund-raising organization — the MMD — a system with a mission (improving the health and life expectancy of children worldwide) but no goal... because it had been achieved!

Rather than disband, MMD became a system in search of a goal. And its board of directors settled on a goal that will likely be "a race without a finish line," at least for the foreseeable future: the elimination of birth defects.

Top to Bottom Visibility

The Goal Tree is a means of fulfilling two of the most important needs of system leaders:

> • Visualizing vertical linkage — how the action "where the rubber meets the road" contributes to the achievement of the system's goal and mission; and

> • Determining what activity is really necessary for system success and what isn't.

The visibility that the Goal Tree contributes also provides another benefit to system leaders: *unity of purpose and focus for the entire organization.* A good Goal Tree allows every member of the organization to see where their efforts fit into the "big picture." When people see this vertical linkage, another interesting phenomenon happens: they understand their own importance to the system's success.

There's an old poem that dates from the American Revolution in the 18th century:

> *For want of a nail, the shoe was lost.*
>
> *For want of a shoe, the horse was lost.*
>
> *For want of a horse, the rider was lost.*
>
> *For want of a rider, the message was lost.*
>
> *For want of a message, the battle was lost.*
>
> *For want of a victory, the war was lost.*
>
> *All for the want of a horseshoe nail.*

In other words, the farrier in the barn—at the lowest level of the organization—gets to see how important his job is to the overall war effort.

Structure of the Goal Tree

As Figure 2.2 indicates, there are three basic components to the Goal Tree: The goal, the critical success factors, and conditions necessary for realizing the critical success factors. There is but one goal at the very top.

The number of critical success factors is limited, usually no more than three to five, as the name "critical success factor" implies. After all, if many things are critical, then the concept of criticality loses its meaning. This begets the need for a specific definition of critical success factors, so that leaders can easily distinguish what's critical and what isn't.

> *Critical Success Factors: That limited set of high-level terminal system outcomes which, collectively, when fulfilled constitute goal attainment.*

Figure 2.3 shows an example of a Goal Tree for the U.S. Naval Air Warfare Center's bombing range at China Lake, California.

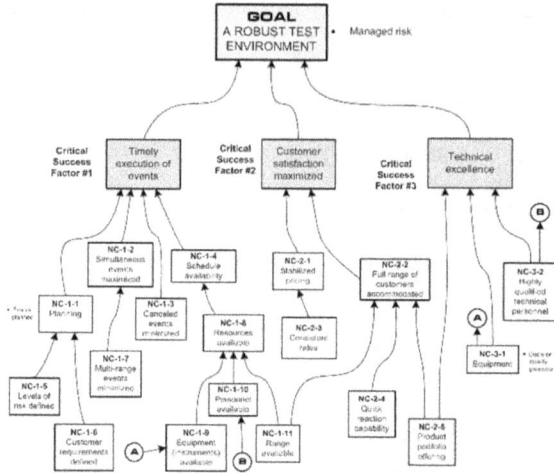

Figure 2.3 – Goal Tree: China Lake Naval Air Weapons Center

Strategy Development and Problem Solving: Two Sides of the Same Coin

It should be clear at this point that the use of a Goal Tree can be a powerful aid in developing strategy. By concentrating management's attention on the desired outcome (mission, goal) and what it takes to achieve that outcome (critical success factors, necessary conditions), it provides the basis of a roadmap for the system. And, after all, what is strategy except a roadmap to the future?

But the Goal Tree has another use, too. While it obviously provides the basis for long term system strategy, it provides a real-time benchmark for current system performance as well. In other words, one can hold up the Goal Tree as a standard for what *should be happening*, the better to identify the places and ways in which it is *not happening*, or at least not to the extent required.

It's been said that a well-defined problem is more than half solved. If your Goal Tree draws your attention immediately to the points in the system where performance is falling short of expectations, then you're well on your way to system improvement. In this mode of application, the Goal Tree serves as the entry point into a comprehensive system-wide analysis leading to creative problem solving. Ultimately, if we characterize the system as a coin, strategy development and complex system problem solving are the obverse and reverse sides. (**Figure 2.5**)

Figure 2.4
Two Sides of
the Same Coin

In the next chapter, we'll see how the Goal Tree starts this problem solving process.

Conclusion

The Goal Tree is the most important logic tree in the Logical Thinking Process. It establishes the entry point for a complex system problem analysis: the benchmark for the performance of the system, regardless of what the purpose of that system might be. This, in turn, ensures that problem-solving efforts are concentrated on the right issues: the ones that will produce maximum tangible improvement in system performance.

But completely independent of the Logical Thinking Process, the Goal Tree can form the basis of a strategy development effort by identifying all the factors related to system success.

> *If you don't have your own plan, someone else is going to make you fit into their plan.*
>
> — *Anthony Robbins* [15]

---

[15] Dettmer. *He Said, She Said*, p.102

Chapter 3.

The Problem Tree (Current Reality Tree)

Complex problems have simple,
easy-to-understand wrong answers.

— Grossman's Misquote of H.L. Mencken [16]

MOST SYSTEMS HAVE SOME SORT OF STRATEGY to get them where they want to be, whether it's formal or not. The smaller the system, the less likely it is to have a formal strategy, and that might not be a bad thing for small systems. But the larger, more complicated the system, the more compelling the need for some kind of structured plan for the future. In large systems, it's generally impossible for anyone to keep all the details and nuances of "directional management" in their heads.

But having a strategy, whether formal or informal, is not enough. As the American cowboy philosopher Will Rogers observed, "Plans get you into things, but you've got to work your own way out." This flash of reality typically impinges on a leader's consciousness when what he or she sees happening is not what they envisioned in the strategy. In other words, reality diverges from the plan. This mismatch between reality and expectations usually creates a kind of disaffection in the mind of the leader: "I can't accept this—I must do something about it!"

The OODA Loop

More often than not, seasoned leaders fall back on their experience and intuition to figure out why the system isn't behaving as expected. **Figure 3.1** depicts the decision process that most

---

[16] Dettmer. *He Said, She Said*, p.105

people intuitively go through, even if they're not conscious of it.[17]

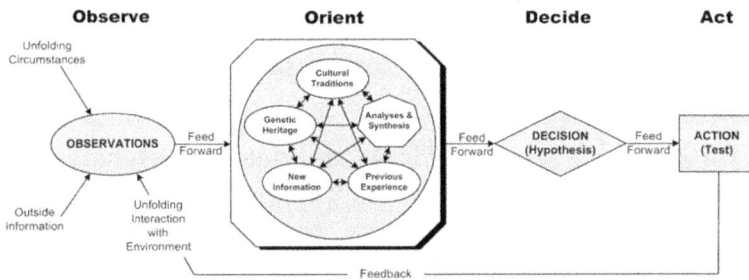

Figure 3.1 – OODA Loop

We OBSERVE what's going on around us, then we ORIENT that observation to our existing knowledge, customs, practices, and understanding of how the world works. The product of this analysis and synthesis is a defined mismatch between what we expect to happen and what we observe is actually happening. This mismatch prompts us to DECIDE what to do to eliminate the mismatch. And finally, we ACT on that decision. What makes this a loop, however, is that we go back and observe the effects of our action on reality: did our action reduce the size of the gap? If so, was it enough? If not, what can we do differently? For most people in our day-to-day lives, this decision process takes place intuitively, often in a matter of seconds.

In many cases, following this loop informally and intuitively works just fine. But in complicated systems operating in complex environments, what appears to be the problem isn't always the end of the story. Often what we actually see is the *effect of a number of underlying causes* that might not be obvious to the casual observer. More often than not, the real underlying cause of this gap between reality and expectations lies several layers of cause-and-effect below the visible level.

---

[17] This figure is referred to as an OODA Loop, which stands for "observe, orient, decide, and act." It was conceived by John R. Boyd, a US Air Force colonel and military strategist, to describe how decisions are made in the confusion and heat of battle. The version offered here is much simplified from the original. SOURCE: http://www.d-n-i.net

Acting on an erroneous conclusion about what's causing the divergence from the strategy can produce even more turbulence in an already beleaguered system, not to mention incurring more unplanned costs. This risk makes it even more critical to ensure that leaders take the right action to close the gap between what *is* and what *should be.*

So, the question becomes: How can I determine what is truly causing the systemic ills that I see happening?

A Problem Tree (Current Reality Tree)

In the preceding chapter, we were introduced to the Goal Tree, which, in effect, establishes our expectations for system performance. "If we accomplish all these necessary conditions, we can satisfy our critical success factors, which in turn will take us to our goal."

It's a relatively simple matter to identify which necessary conditions are falling short of expectations and which critical success factors are compromised. It not so easy, however, to know why these shortcomings are happening. Moreover, if the visible performance deficiencies result from failures at a deeper level—one that isn't immediately obvious to casual observation—we risk assuming the wrong cause is at work and taking action that is either ineffective or creates more, newer problems than it solves.

Fortunately, the Logical Thinking Process comes with a component that resolves this issue: a Problem Tree.[18] This tool fits seamlessly in with Boyd's Orient step in the OODA loop. Refer to **Figure 3.2**.

---

[18] This logical tool is also referred to as a Current Reality Tree, because it depicts the interactive cause and effect of the real world as it is happening now.

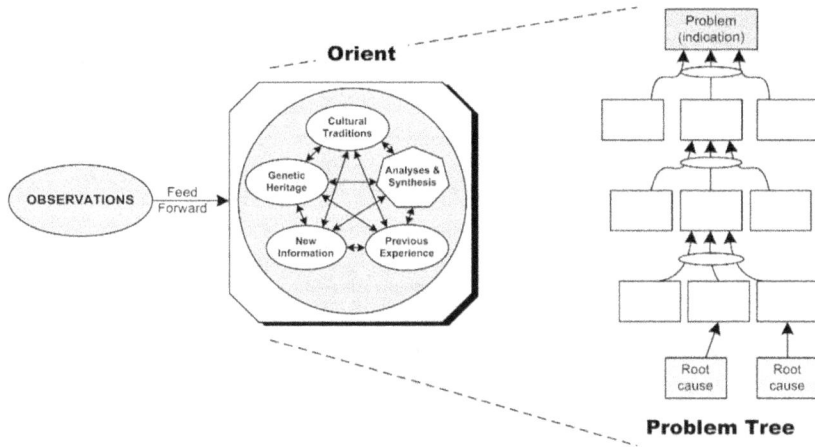

Figure 3.2 OODA Loop and Problem Tree

A conscious effort to observe and gather information from the external environment, combined with organized internal data and information collection, provides the "raw material" for the Orient step. The many-sided cross-referencing of gathered information with current customs and practices, existing knowledge, cultural traditions, and previous experience takes place in the body of the Problem Tree.

Following a relatively straightforward set of instructions, all of those inputs are analyzed and synthesized into an accurate picture of what's happening within the system (and between the system and its operating environment) now.

The Problem Tree is really a "negative" tree. It doesn't depict *all* of reality. It only reflects that part of existing reality that isn't performing the way we'd like. To that extent, it could be considered *management by exception*: it shows us that aspect of reality that isn't meeting our expectations, and only at those times when it isn't doing so if it's intermittent.

The very top of a Problem Tree displays the visible indication of the divergence between expectations and reality. This is a grammatical statement that is termed an *undesirable effect*, in recognition of the fact that it's the end result of a chain of cause and effect, not the origin.

Figure 3.3 shows a simple Problem Tree. Notice that the use of complete sentences makes it easy to read and follow the logic. You begin with the blocks at the bottom of the tree and follow the arrows vertically to the top reading...

"If ... [first cause] and [contributing cause]... then [immediate effect]."

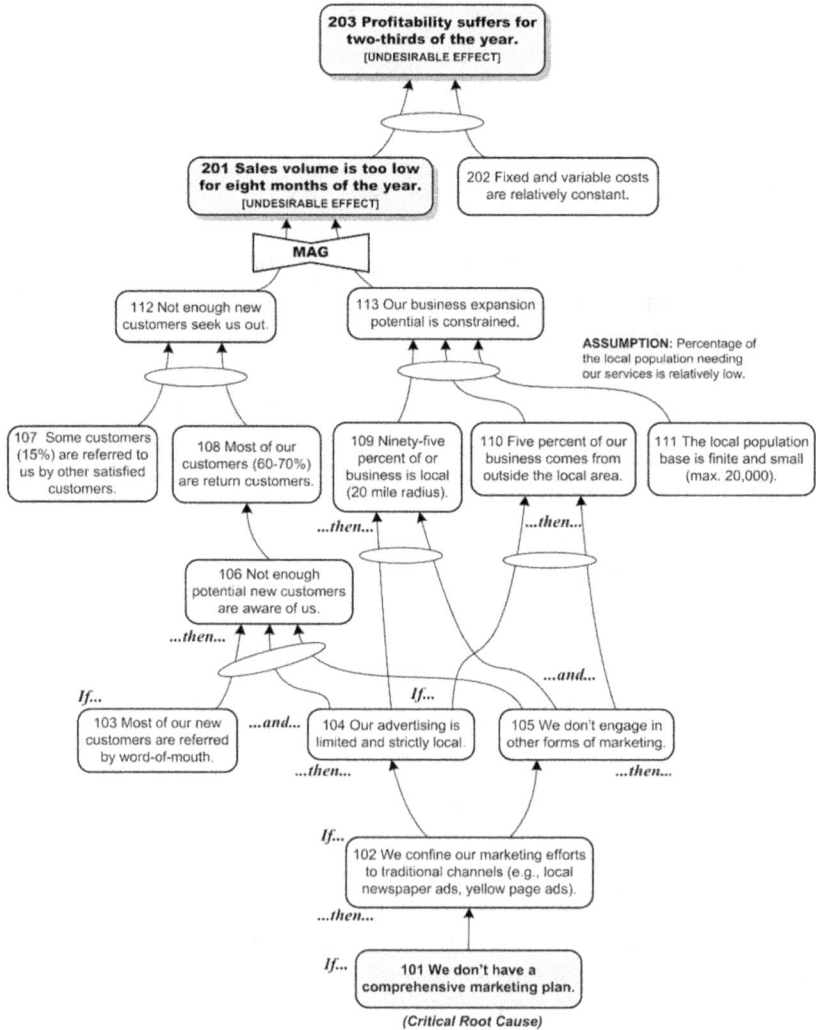

203 Profitability suffers for two-thirds of the year.
[UNDESIRABLE EFFECT]

201 Sales volume is too low for eight months of the year.
[UNDESIRABLE EFFECT]

202 Fixed and variable costs are relatively constant.

MAG

112 Not enough new customers seek us out.

113 Our business expansion potential is constrained.

ASSUMPTION: Percentage of the local population needing our services is relatively low.

107 Some customers (15%) are referred to us by other satisfied customers.

108 Most of our customers (60-70%) are return customers.

109 Ninety-five percent of or business is local (20 mile radius).

110 Five percent of our business comes from outside the local area.

111 The local population base is finite and small (max. 20,000).

...then...

...then...

106 Not enough potential new customers are aware of us.

...then...

...and...

If...

103 Most of our new customers are referred by word-of-mouth.

...and...

If...

104 Our advertising is limited and strictly local.

105 We don't engage in other forms of marketing.

...then...

...then...

If...

102 We confine our marketing efforts to traditional channels (e.g., local newspaper ads, yellow page ads).

...then...

If...

101 We don't have a comprehensive marketing plan.

(Critical Root Cause)

Figure 3.3 Problem Tree (Example)

The immediate effect then becomes the cause of the next layer of effect. For simplicity's sake, Figure 3.3 has "If...," "...and...," and "...then..." included part of the way to show how to read the blocks. Normally, a Problem Tree won't show that.

Notice a couple of things about Figure 3.3. The first is that the statements are all complete sentences in plain language. This makes reading the Problem Tree simple for most people and highly intuitive. Second, it adheres to a structured if-then format which becomes familiar and easy to use very quickly. In other words, it communicates well.

Third, and not so obvious, the statements and if-then connections in the tree impose a rigorous sense of logic on the message being communicated. This doesn't happen by itself. This logical progression is informed and structured by adherence to a set of eight basic rules of logic.

The Rules of Logic

CLARITY – The complete understanding of what has been said

ENTITY EXISTENCE – The provable validity of a statement

CAUSALITY EXISTENCE – The cause, as stated, leads directly and unavoidably to the stated effect

CAUSE INSUFFICIENCY – The cause, as stated, is not sufficient alone to produce the stated effect

ADDITIONAL CAUSE – Another completely independent cause can produce the same effect

CAUSE-EFFECT REVERSAL – The cause, as stated is actually the effect, and the effect, as stated, is actually the cause

PREDICTED EFFECT EXISTENCE – One or more additional, verifiable effects result from the same cause

TAUTOLOGY – The effect is offered as the rationale for the existence of the cause (circular reasoning)

The net results of structuring the Problem Tree according to logical rules, and expressing the message of the tree in complete sentences, is that it *provides and effectively communicates common sense.* [19]

Anyone familiar with the situation expressed in the tree can read and understand it without much explanation beyond "Start at the bottom, read 'if,' 'and,' and 'then,' and stop at the top." It doesn't get much simpler than that.

Conclusion

The Goal Tree answers the question "What *should* we be achieving?" The Problem Tree answers two further questions:

What is *actually* happening in our system?

Why is it *not* what we intended?

Notice that nowhere is *what to do* about the situation mentioned. That's because this phase of the Logical Thinking Process is devoted to effectively defining the true nature of the problem. A well defined problem is more than half solved. And solving our problem begins with the next phase: the Conflict Resolution Diagram. We'll see how that works in the next chapter.

> *Almost anything is easier to get into than to get out of.*
>
> — *Allen's Law* [20]

---

[19] It's important to note that these eight rules of logic govern critical thinking and reasoning of _any_ kind, not just LTP logic tree construction.
[20] Dettmer. *He Said, She Said*, p.106

Chapter 4.
Conflict Resolution (Evaporating Cloud)

*The compromise will always be more expensive
than either of the suggestions it is compromising.*

— Juhani's Law [21]

CONFLICT HAS ALWAYS BEEN an endemic part of human existence. Whether it's war among nations, fighting between individuals, or merely differences of opinion, conflict seems to be in the
nature of mankind. So, why should we be surprised when conflict features so prominently in interpersonal or business rela-
tions?

What makes conflict such a problem in human systems is
probably best described as *friction*. Picture a machine — an automobile, for instance. As it moves along a highway at cruising
speed, a high throttle setting is required to maintain speed. If we
let up on the accelerator, friction within the transmission and
wheel bearings starts the speed decaying. This deceleration is
amplified by the rolling friction between the tires and the road.
Eventually, if we don't apply the accelerator again, the car
grinds to a full stop. Friction has brought it to a halt.

Likewise, in systems the friction of conflict can slow progress
down, even bringing it to a halt. This conflict need not be overt,
such as in a direct argument between two people. It could be no
more than a strongly held difference of opinion. But if even two
people whose performance is essential to success actively disa-
gree, then progress is slowed and success is at risk.

Perhaps the most sensitive conflict in human systems is related to change. People like the familiar, and changing the way

---

[21] Dettmer. *He Said, She Said*, p.30.

they do things upsets familiarity. It causes mental or emotional discomfort, which most people tend to shy away from. As a result, people whose comfort depends on predictability tend to push back against change. (**Figure 4.1**)

Frank and Ernest

Figure 4.1 - Resistance to Change

FRANK & ERNEST © 1975 Thaves, Used By permission of ANDREWS MCMEEL SYNDICATION. All rights reserved.

Change and the Logical Thinking Process

The Logical Thinking Process was originally designed to solve complicated problems, as explained in Chapter 1. The crux of solving such problems is changing the status quo. After all, if you always do what you've always done, you'll always get what you've always gotten. But everybody's "improvement" is somebody else's "change" — and change is not always viewed favorably. As Machiavelli once noted:

> *Nothing is more difficult to carry out, nor more doubtful of success, nor more dangerous to handle, than to initiate a new order of things. For the reformer has enemies in all those who profit by the old order, and only lukewarm defenders in all those who would profit by the new order, this lukewarmness arising partly from ... the incredulity of mankind, who do not truly believe in anything new until they have had actual experience in it.*

> *— Niccolò Machiavelli* [22]

Put these two phenomena together — friction and skepticism about change — and you have a sure-fire formula for failure. Or at least stagnation.

---

[22] Dettmer. *He Said, She Said.* P.17.

The Conflict Resolution Diagram (Evaporating Cloud)

Let's assume that we've just completed a Problem Tree on a significant issue hindering the system's march toward its goal. Let's also say that once we identify the root causes of the problem, it's pretty clear that it's going to be difficult to remove (or change) them. Someone, maybe many people, with a stake in the status quo will oppose changing things. We've all heard that reaction verbalized: "Boy, that's going to be a hard sell. So-and-so won't sit still for *that!*"

On the one hand, we know that if we can make the change successfully, things will rapidly get better. On the other hand, we know that if we don't change, they won't. What can we do?

First, we can recognize that this dilemma — this indecision, uncertainty, or hesitation — is the quintessential characterization of a conflict, even if there are no harsh words, recalcitrant behavior, or other overt signs of contention. Second, we can apply the next tree in the Logical Thinking Process — the Conflict Resolution Diagram — with more than a little confidence that it can help us work through the situation effectively.

Win-Win

Conflicts can be resolved in three ways. The resolution can be imposed, usually by some party with substantial power. The two sides can compromise, in which case neither side gets what they want (at least not fully). Or, they can attempt to work out a resolution in which both sides are fully satisfied. The primary obstacle to this last approach is ignorance:

- People may not understand what *the other side* really wants and why

- They may not fully understand what *they* want and why, and ...

- They don't know how to go about the process of crafting a "win" for both sides.

Fortunately, the Conflict Resolution Diagram can provide the ways to overcome all three of these obstacles. And it does so by engaging the opposite side of the conflict in a conscientious effort to jointly resolve the contention in a way that both sides can readily accept.

What Does a Conflict Look Like When It's Structured for Resolution?

The full presentation of a conflict for resolution requires five elements: an *objective*, two *requirements* for achieving that objective, and two *prerequisites* for satisfying those requirements. These elements are connected together in a five-sided geometric figure that looks like **Figure 4.2**.

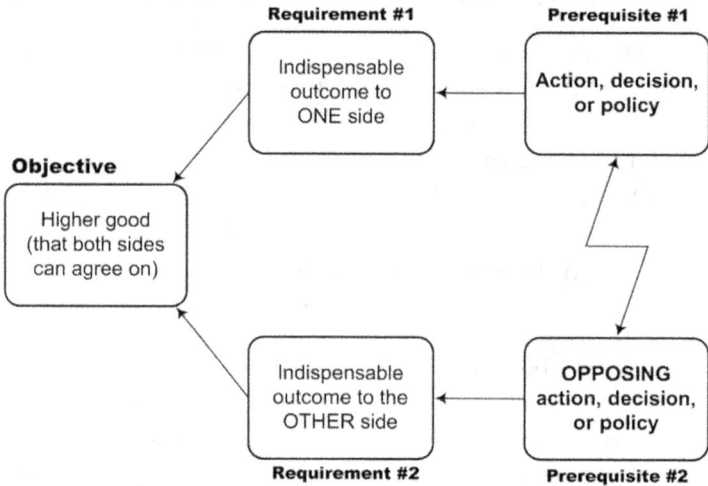

Requirement #1

Indispensable outcome to ONE side

Prerequisite #1

Action, decision, or policy

Objective

Higher good (that both sides can agree on)

Requirement #2

Indispensable outcome to the OTHER side

Prerequisite #2

OPPOSING action, decision, or policy

Figure 4.2 Conflict Structure

On the right side, we have the two contending positions in the conflict. These are inevitably some kind of action or decision which that side wants to see taken. Or they may be a policy of some kind: one side wants to see the policy changed, the other side wants to see it remain the same. These actions, etc., are referred to as "prerequisites," because each side perceives them to be essential to achieving their desired, higher-level outcome.

These higher-level outcomes are requirements which are assumed to be satisfied by the accomplishment of the prerequisites. Notice the use of the word "assumed." This implies that we take as fact the idea that doing the action actually does produce the requirement. As we'll see when we explore ways to resolve the conflict, this is not always the case—maybe not even most of the time.

It's important to note that the two requirements are not in conflict with one another. If they truly are requirements, then by definition they *can't* be in conflict with one another.[23]

Finally, on the left side we find the common objective of each side in the conflict. For conflicts that reside within the same system, there will always be some common objective of the contending sides. If this doesn't seem to be the case, then either the wrong objective has been assumed or the stated objective is not really at least *one systemic level* above the two requirements in the hierarchy.

An Example

These abstract concepts become more real when we see a practical example. Let's consider a typical systemic conflict and see how it might be framed in a Conflict Resolution Diagram for easy solution.

In our example, the system will be a for-profit commercial company. (It might just as easily have been a not-for-profit organization or a government agency.)

The company produces some kind of product or service for sale to the public. It's the sale of this product or service that delivers the company's profits. But at the moment, perhaps owing to economic conditions, sales are significantly below expectations, and have been for several months. Much of the work force has been idle ... but they still represent a cost to the system, even though few sales are coming in to offset that cost.

The general manager of the company is on the horns of a dilemma. On one hand, he or she feels pressure to take action to improve short-term profitability. The obvious (to the manager)

---

[23] If you think that two requirements are, in fact, in conflict with one another, it may well be that either or both of them are not really system requirements, but rather operational policies... which are eligible to be changed. If that's the case, then they can't really be non-negotiable requirements.

choice is to reduce non-productive costs by laying off underutilized employees. On the other hand, the manager knows that if sales turn around dramatically, there won't be enough qualified workers available to provide satisfactory service or product to the customers.

The Conflict Resolution Diagram

The general manager's dilemma is illustrated in **Figure 4.3**, below:

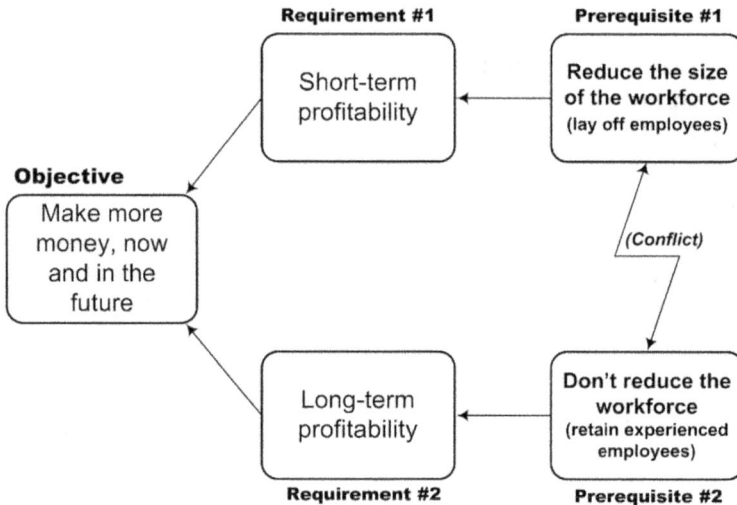

Requirement #1

Short-term profitability

Prerequisite #1

Reduce the size of the workforce (lay off employees)

Objective

Make more money, now and in the future

(Conflict)

Long-term profitability

Don't reduce the workforce (retain experienced employees)

Requirement #2

Prerequisite #2

Figure 4.3 – Short v. Long Term

This graphical representation is called a Conflict Resolution Diagram. Simplified to its essence, and read from left to right, the conflict sounds like this:

In order to make more money, now and in the future... I must achieve short-term profitability. I must also realize long-term profitability.

In order to achieve short-term profitability, I <u>must reduce</u> the size of the workforce.

In order to realize long-term profitability, I <u>must not reduce</u> the size of the workforce.

I can't do both at the same time.

This is about as simply and concisely as a conflict can be stated. Once the conflict is articulated this way, however, it's easy for people on both sides to agree that it's an accurate expression of the essence of the conflict. Now the question becomes, "What do we do about it?"

The first thing we should do is to recognize that the Conflict Resolution Diagram doesn't necessarily represent reality. It only *implies our assumptions* about reality. What does this mean?

Just that, as far as we can see at the moment, we *think* it's an accurate representation of the situation. We *assume* that it is, absent any evidence to the contrary. But we must recognize that we might well be wrong. In fact, effective conflict resolution *depends* on the idea that, concerning at least some aspects of the conflict, we *are* wrong. That makes it up to us to look for evidence to the contrary, to find out where our errors in thinking lie. In other words, we must challenge our assumptions and root out our *invalid ones* about the way things are, or must be.

Invalid Assumptions

If you stop to examine all the significant conflicts in human history, from wars all the way down to individual arguments, I submit that you will find most of them to be founded on mistaken assumptions. These could be mistaken assumptions about things that other people have done, or that we think must be done. Or they could be misunderstandings about motivations, or any number of other similar errors.

However, if we act on (or continue acting on) these erroneous assumptions, eventually we'll encounter some kind of "cognitive dissonance": someone will resist us for no apparent good reason, or we'll find ourselves locked into some unpleasant "either-or" situation. But if we're able to find the errors in our own thinking, or that of others, then the door is open to one side or the other to change their minds about the conflict.

The key, then, is to *find the invalid assumptions that perpetuate the conflict*. To do that effectively, though, we must expose as many assumptions about both sides of the conflict as possible ...

and then identify from among them the ones that are invalid or not relevant.

In a logic tree such as the Conflict Resolution Diagram, every arrow represents underlying, unstated assumptions. Our challenge is to draw them out. This is typically an effort that benefits from "having brainpower thrown at it." In other words, engage several knowledgeable, well-intended people in the task.

Let's say that we've done that in our example. **Figure 4.4** shows some typical assumptions associated with each side of this particular conflict.[24]

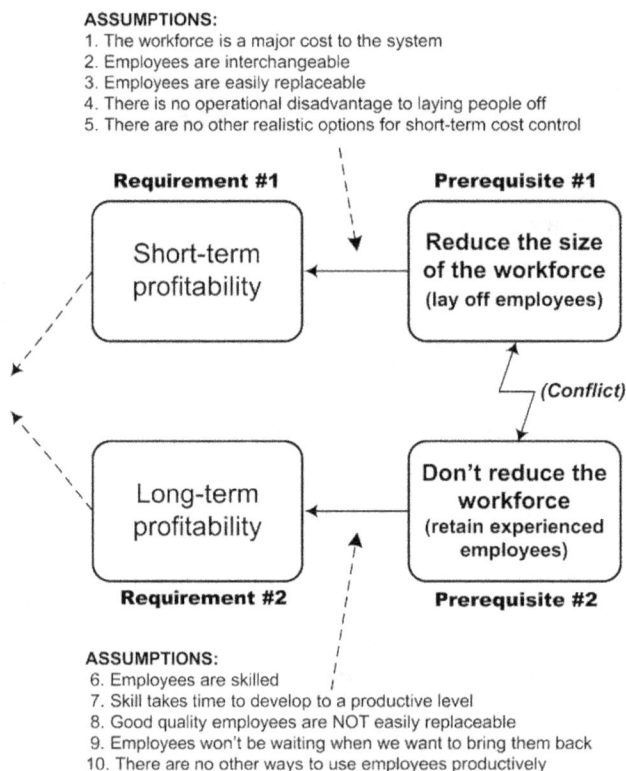

ASSUMPTIONS:
1. The workforce is a major cost to the system
2. Employees are interchangeable
3. Employees are easily replaceable
4. There is no operational disadvantage to laying people off
5. There are no other realistic options for short-term cost control

Requirement #1   **Prerequisite #1**

Short-term profitability   **Reduce the size of the workforce** (lay off employees)

(Conflict)

Long-term profitability   **Don't reduce the workforce** (retain experienced employees)

Requirement #2   **Prerequisite #2**

ASSUMPTIONS:
6. Employees are skilled
7. Skill takes time to develop to a productive level
8. Good quality employees are NOT easily replaceable
9. Employees won't be waiting when we want to bring them back
10. There are no other ways to use employees productively

Figure 4.4 – Assumptions

---

[24] These are assumptions are by no means a complete list. There are undoubtedly many more that might apply but aren't stated here. I provide these only for illustration.

Even from a casual glance at these assumptions, it should be obvious that some (not all) are highly questionable, at the very least. Some might be outright wrong.

The point is that the questionable or wrong assumptions are the "gateway" to breaking the conflict. They provide the impetus to say, "Wait a minute—that's not right!" And from there, it's an easy step to envisioning alternatives to one of the two prerequisites. As soon as we find an acceptable, practical alternative to one of the contending positions, the conflict is neutralized ... and in a manner that enables each side to satisfy its non-negotiable requirement.

Conflict Solutions

The alternative—the "third way"—that dissolves the conflict is referred to as an *injection*, because it's something new that we must inject into the situation. It doesn't exist now. From a practical perspective, in many situations it's unlikely that a single such change (injection) will completely resolve the conflict. Two or more might be required, but the number will normally be finite and manageable. **Figure 4.5** shows examples of several injections which, when linked together, might provide a workable way to *effect cost control without sacrificing employees*. In other words, they replace the prerequisite "Reduce the size of the workforce."

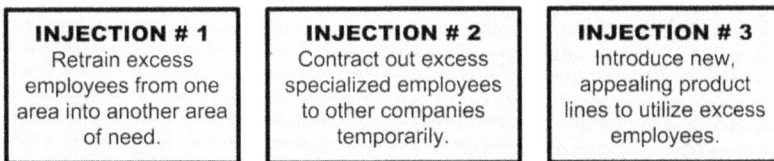

INJECTION # 1	**INJECTION # 2**	**INJECTION # 3**
Retrain excess employees from one area into another area of need.	Contract out excess specialized employees to other companies temporarily.	Introduce new, appealing product lines to utilize excess employees.

Figure 4.5 – Injections

The injections in Figure 4.5 are merely examples. They might not be feasible in all circumstances, but there may well be others that are. The point is that coming up with injections—ideas for a solution to the conflict—is a creative exercise based on the presumption that either or both of the conflicting prerequisites in the Conflict Resolution Diagram is not really absolutely necessary for attainment of the overall objective. In other words, there's more than one way to skin a cat ... and you don't necessarily have to throw away either the cat or the skin afterward!

"Find out *exactly* how many ways there are to skin a cat."

Conclusion

Any systemic change is likely to elicit some degree of push-back, and perhaps even outright resistance. Even people without formal authority may have the capability to "slow-roll" or even frustrate successful change. Determining a systemic root cause that should be changed might only be half the battle. But fortunately the Logical Thinking Process provides a component that can help break that "logjam."

A good compromise leaves everybody mad.

— Unknown [25]

---

[25] Dettmer. *He Said, She Said*, p.30

CHAPTER 5.

The Solution Tree (Future Reality Tree)

The chief cause of problems is solutions.

— Sevareid's Law [26]

HOW MANY TIMES HAVE YOU SEEN (or experienced) a situation in which people recognize a problem and jump immediately to a solution? The classic case in business is lower-than-expected income in a particular quarter. The executive committee sees this reported by the chief financial officer, and someone says, "Well, obviously we have to cut costs!" No cause-effect analysis, just start "shooting in the dark." This type of behavior results from inadequate or no effort at rational problem solving to begin with. In many systems, the best that people can come up with is a "seat-of-the-pants" approach to solving problems. (See **Figure 5.1**)

However, even when a problem is thoroughly analyzed and the cause accurately defined, it's often very tempting to grasp instinctively at a solution without considering its implications. This can be very risky. And if the problem is large and complicated, it can result in a serious waste of time, money and manpower without making much of a dent in the problem.

There are two potential pitfalls in not adopting a logical approach to solving a complicated problem.

1. The solution developed and agreed upon may not actually do much, if anything, to solve the problem.

2. The solution may create new, unanticipated problems that are as bad or worse than the original one.

---

[26] Dettmer. *He Said, She Said*, p.114.

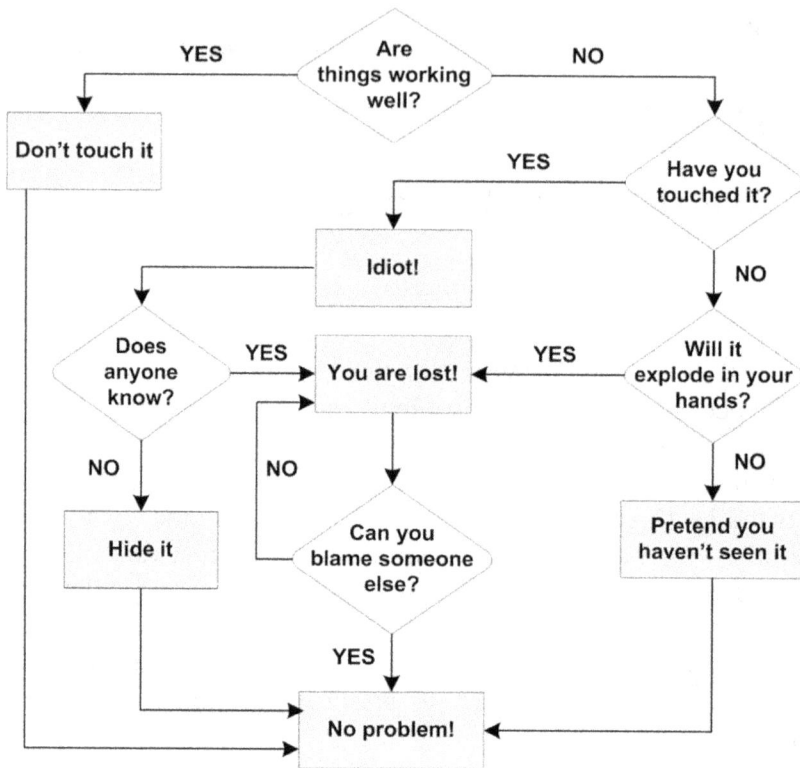

Figure 5.1 – Problem-solving Flowchart

Ineffective Problem Solving

Perhaps the worst thing we can do in trying to overcome problems is to chase after a solution that turns out to be ineffective. Most of us have seen that in one form or another.

Commercially, consider, for example companies like Kodak and Blockbuster Video, which fell from the heights into bankruptcy because they were unable to figure out how to manage a rapidly changing competitive environment. And then there was Coca Cola's plunge into "New Coke" in the 1980s, which turned into a monumental debacle.

From a financial standpoint, the US Federal government is even worse, with ideas such as the electronic benefit transfer card system that hemorrhages taxpayer money through fraud and insane expenditures on projects such as Solyndra, which sucked half a billion taxpayer dollars down a dark hole. Then there are the failed concepts of shovel-ready jobs and static scoring of revenue impact of tax reduction. (The government is too fertile a field for such disasters.)

As individuals go, there is no limit to the mistakes people commit in problem solving and decision making (which are closely related). The 2016 US Presidential election needs no introduction, on either side, a misplaced (perhaps fatal) dependence on opioid drugs, and choices in a career or a mate come to mind.

It's possible to overcome such errors, at any of the aforementioned levels. Money and manpower can generally be reconstituted. But time is the one irreplaceable commodity. Even if we can absorb the waste of money and diversion of manpower from other activities, we can never recover the time we lose pursuing a solution that ends up not working.

Worse Problems

It often seems that in trying to solve one problem, we create new, potentially worse ones. For example, pharmaceutical science created antibiotics to save untold millions from the depredations of bacterial infection. But in doing so, the medical community came to see antibiotics as a universal cure. Doctors would prescribe them when not really needed, "just to be safe." The net result was overuse of antibiotics, causing the rise of stronger bacteria more resistant to antibiotics. This became a vicious cycle (what we refer to in the Logical Thinking Process as a *negative reinforcing loop*). Later strains of bacteria are largely impervious to the antibiotics currently available.

Or consider the development of mobile/cellular telephones. Their evolution into a computer-and-Internet-in-your-pocket provided all manner of improvements to life and benefits to mankind. But at the same time, injuries and fatalities increased resulting from people not seeing impending danger, because their attention was "buried" in their mobile phones. Moreover, now many people are incapable of doing basic tasks because they depend so heavily on their portable digital devices.

A Subtle Penalty

There is an insidious effect of ill-considered problem solutions, too: The human toll. Any so-called improvement is someone's change, and change is not always welcome to many people. In fact, some avoid it like the plague. Why?

Because it upsets people's "comfortable" ways of doing things. It creates turbulence, and turbulence can cause stress. The health impacts of stress are well documented, but even if very few people suffer stress-related health problems, their efficiency after the change may suffer for some undetermined length of time. People find comfort and confidence in the familiar ways to doing things, discomfort and uncertainty in new ways.

Perhaps the most insidious risk of all is passive resistance. If people are upset enough about change, they may look for ways to make the change fail, in hopes that leaders will write off the effort as a bad idea and revert to the way things were. Everybody in any system is a potential Gandhi: they have some power to frustrate changes by deliberate inaction or half-hearted effort.

The Solution (Future Reality) Tree

The Logical Thinking Process provides a way to develop and test solutions to problems defined in a Problem Tree. The Solution Tree (originally referred to as a Future Reality Tree) uses the same logical approach and structure, but rather than looking backward or toward the present, it seeks to delineate *future* cause and effect. Basically, it poses the question:

> *If we take this action to solve our problem, what can we expect the ultimate outcome to be?*

The answer provided in the Solution Tree is two-fold. First, it can tell you whether or not your proposed course of action will, in fact, deliver the results you desire. And it will demonstrate through tight logic that the results you hope to achieve are attainable. Alternatively, your Solution Tree might bring you to the edge of a cliff (with your desired outcome on the other side of an impassable gap). In this case, the effort hasn't been wasted; it has actually saved you from committing to an unproductive cure to your problem.

Thomas Edison, one of the world's most famous inventors once said, "I have not failed 10,000 times. I have successfully found 10,000 ways that will not work." [27] But Edison's approach to invention was trial and error. That might have been acceptable when he was inventing the incandescent electric light, but few of us can afford the luxury of trial and error today. Fortunately, with the Solution Tree we reduce the risk of failure to a manageable level ahead of time.

Second, the Solution Tree can help you avoid creating newer, possibly worse problems than you had to begin with. It achieves this through the deliberate use of a subroutine in the Solution Tree known as the Negative Branch.[28] The Negative Branch answers the question, "Besides reaching our desired outcome, what new, potentially devastating effects might our choice of solutions have?"

With these two capabilities in a leader's arsenal—the ability to logically prove that your proposed change will give you the results you want, and the assurance that it won't cause newer, more aggravating problems than it solves—it becomes possible to press on in a new direction with confidence that "we're doing the right thing."

Solution Tree: An Example

What does a Solution Tree look like? Pretty much what a Problem Tree looks like. (See **Figure 5.2**) The crucial difference is that the Solution Tree is *not representing established fact*. It's depicting a future that does not yet exist. So, it really reflects *probability*, rather than reality. The logic and the connections are the same, and some of the contributing causes may be established

---

[27] Dettmer. *He Said, She Said*. p.40.
[28] A Negative Branch differs from a Negative *Reinforcing Loop*. The former is an element of the Problem Tree. It explains why a situation seems to get worse on its own. The Negative *Branch* is a projection into the future of what could go wrong if a particular course of action is adopted.

facts. But the outcome of the Solution Tree—the Desired Effects at the top—are *predictions* of what is most likely to happen as a result of the actions taken at the bottom.

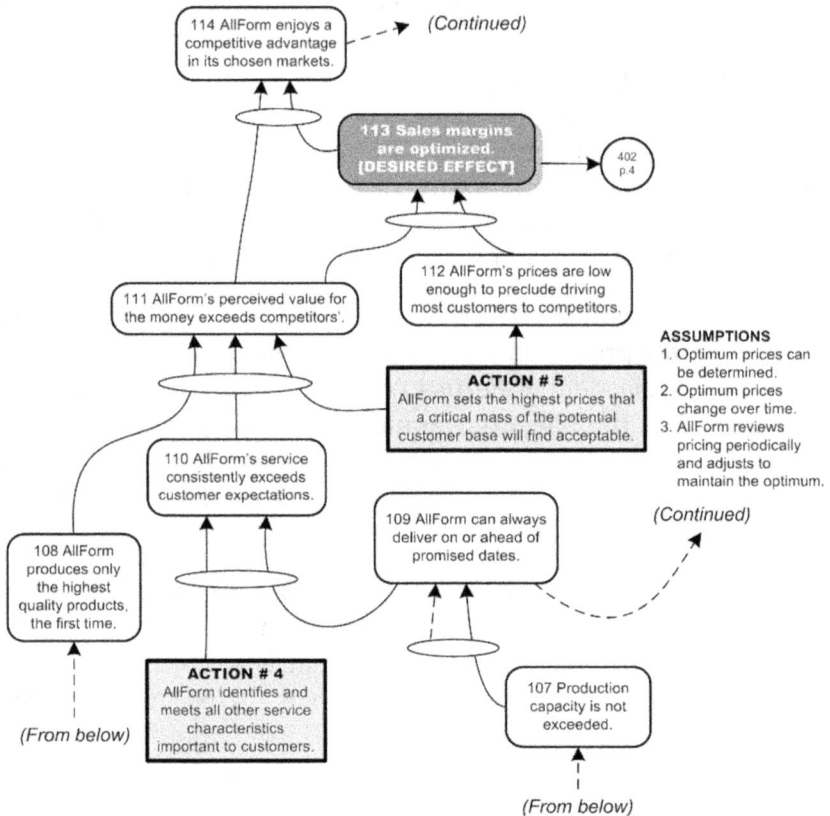

114 AllForm enjoys a competitive advantage in its chosen markets.

(Continued)

113 Sales margins are optimized. [DESIRED EFFECT]

402 p.4

112 AllForm's prices are low enough to preclude driving most customers to competitors.

111 AllForm's perceived value for the money exceeds competitors'.

ACTION # 5
AllForm sets the highest prices that a critical mass of the potential customer base will find acceptable.

ASSUMPTIONS
1. Optimum prices can be determined.
2. Optimum prices change over time.
3. AllForm reviews pricing periodically and adjusts to maintain the optimum.

110 AllForm's service consistently exceeds customer expectations.

109 AllForm can always deliver on or ahead of promised dates.

(Continued)

108 AllForm produces only the highest quality products, the first time.

ACTION # 4
AllForm identifies and meets all other service characteristics important to customers.

107 Production capacity is not exceeded.

(From below)

(From below)

Figure 5.2 AllForm Solution Tree (partial)

This prediction of probability can be highly dependable, providing that the statements are based of verifiable evidence, known laws of physics, or deep intuition—in other words, deep subject matter *knowledge*.

Strategic Planning and the Solution Tree

Personally, I find the Solution Tree to be my favorite of all the Logical Thinking Process tools. If it hasn't occurred to you by now, I should point out that a well-developed Solution Tree can be the basis of a strategic roadmap to a system's future. And I can think of nothing more exciting—and fulfilling!—than plotting a course into the future, confident that I can achieve my ultimate goal. It would not be an exaggeration to say that designing a system's future with a Solution Tree[29] is truly a creative effort.

> *Long-range planning does not deal with future decisions, but with the future of present decisions.*
>
> *— Peter F. Drucker* [30]

---

[29] Using a Solution Tree in this mode—to create a system's future—justifies the use of the original name of this tool: Future Reality Tree.

[30] Dettmer. *He Said, She Said*, p.102.

Chapter 6.
The Deployment Tree (Prerequisite Tree)

The world cares very little about what a man or woman knows. It is what the man or woman is able to do that counts.

— Booker T. Washington [31]

FELIPE PABLO MARTINEZ ONCE SAID that the bright guys are all drinking espresso in cafés, discussing how the world should be. The dumb guys are all back in the office, changing the world.[32] This observation emphasizes the fact that great ideas don't always make effective solutions. In many cases, they don't even make it to *being* solutions. In the preceding chapter, we saw that the first criterion for a good solution to a complex system problem is that there must be some verification that it will actually work—that it will do what it's intended to do.

But even a verified idea is no more than potential energy. Converting it to kinetic energy requires action of some kind. Unfortunately, when it comes to executing ideas that might have a lot of "moving parts," solutions can fall apart. A new symphony can look great on paper, but it requires competent musicians to actually play the notes. And it requires an inspired conductor to lead the orchestra, interpret the composer's score, and coordinate the performance of the different orchestral sections. In other words, *it's all in the execution.*

Execution Planning

It's no different when it comes to making important but complicated changes in systems: once the effectiveness of the

---

[31] Dettmer. *He Said, She Said*, p.16.
[32] Dettmer. *He Said, She Said*, p.13.

change is validated, somebody has to do *something* about making it happen. But as we all know, it's often difficult to know where to start. Consider the proposal to construct a new corporate facility—a complicated undertaking, indeed. But any such complicated task can usually be accomplished confidently and effectively with the help of an execution plan. In the case of a facility, a construction plan is an integral part. It details how the land will be cleared and prepared, the laying of the foundation, the erection of the structure, installation of electric utilities and plumbing, and finishing of the interior.

But there's more than just construction to consider. An execution plan also prescribes how the logistics will be set up for the new operations to take place there, when the equipment and supplies will be installed and delivered, and even how the staff will be hired and trained.

Clearly, all of this doesn't happen simultaneously. Everyone would be tripping over one another. So, the execution plan details not only *what* must be done, but also in *what sequence*. And it invariably establishes who is responsible for doing what, as well.

Project Management

Typically, complicated changes or developments are managed as projects, using traditional (and even new) project management techniques and tools. The implementation of a new data management system, SAP for example, is a typical "idea for a solution" that might be managed as a project, even though it may not require brick-and-mortar construction.

But even a non-construction effort, formally managed as a project, requires two things: 1) the delineation of all required tasks to be performed, and 2) the sequence (dependency) in which they must occur. Certainly, projects all have the parameters of performance, cost, and schedule. But they begin with *what must be done and in what sequence*. This is not always clear to everyone involved.

Deployment

Regardless of the complexity, deployment of a new idea— action—begins with identification of *what must be done and in what sequence.* Even if the idea is as informal as a company Christmas party or as complicated as an international conference, these two functions are the first step in deployment.

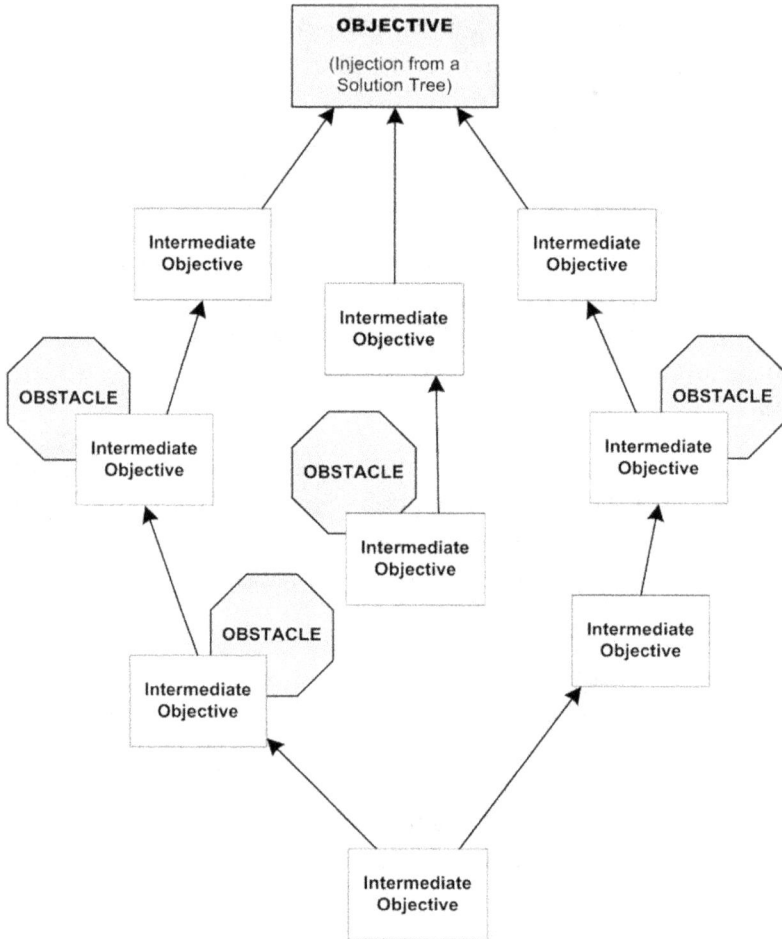

Figure 6.1 – Deployment Tree (generic)

The Logical Thinking Process offers a handy way to begin that transition from idea to operation. It's a Deployment Tree, also referred to as a Prerequisite Tree.33 While "prerequisite" is an accurate characteristic, we refer to it here as a Deployment Tree, because that's what its ultimate function is: deployment, or execution, of some new idea — frequently a change of some kind. The Deployment Tree looks like this (See **Figure 6.1**).

Peeling an Onion

The Deployment Tree is limited in scope. It's designed to address only the specific tasks or accomplishments needed to achieve one very specific objective. All are precisely defined. There is no doubt in anyone's mind what is required to complete them. We're no longer working at the problem definition or solution level — we're working at the *action* level.

The completion of each task leads to the commencement of the next, until all component tasks required to achieve the stated objective are completed. All tasks located *higher in the tree* are addressed *later in the process*, closer to the time the overall objective is achieved. So, reading the tree from the top down is somewhat like peeling an onion, starting with the last layer "grown" and ending with the first one "started." This sequential progression makes preceding tasks *prerequisites* of the later ones. This is how the Deployment Tree earned its original name: *Prerequisite Tree*.

Sequence and Parallel

The preceding analogy with peeling an onion implies a *sequence* of events. A subsequent task can't be started until the preceding task is finished. Usually, this is because the outcome of a completed task is at least one entering argument for the discharge of the next one.

However, not all tasks in a Deployment Tree are in a single sequential line. Especially in more complicated projects, there

---

33 Also called a Prerequisite Tree because its structure is made up of individual, discrete tasks that must be accomplished in sequence as prerequisites to achieving the final objective at the top.

may be several separate sequential tasks that intersect or eventually merge with one another before completion. This is typical in hardware or software development projects. (See **Figure 6.2**)

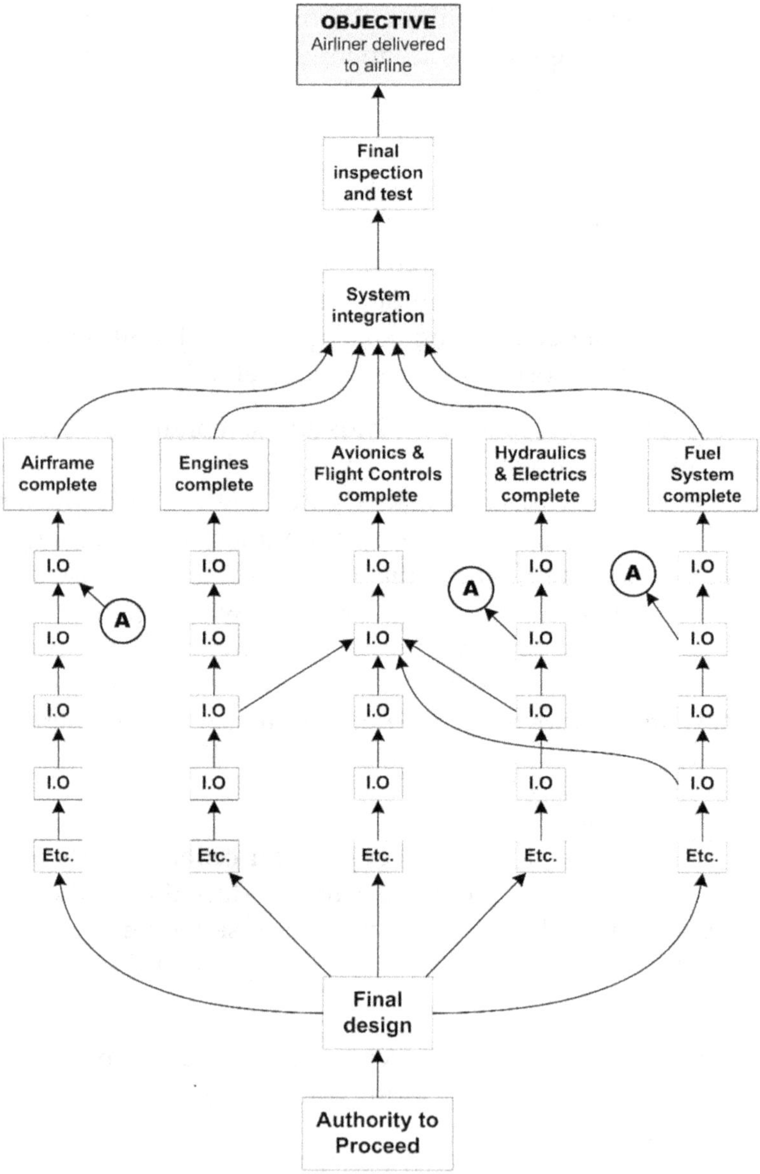

Figure 6.2 – Deployment Tree (project)

Notice that this diagram looks suspiciously like a project activity network, which might be the basis of a PERT/ CPM or Critical Chain chart. Guilty as charged! A Deployment Tree has essentially the same structure as a project activity network — which should make it obvious that a Deployment Tree could be used to define the structure and sequence of tasks for a formal project. That's not its only use, but it *is* an important one.

It's important to remember, however, that the Deployment Tree was not originally conceived to execute projects. It was designed to help change agents and system leaders figure out how to overcome obstacles to taking action of some kind. The Deployment Tree in Figure 6.2 indicates no obstacles, because it's intended for formal project execution. In most cases, you would use a Deployment Tree to map out how you might accomplish something you (or your system) had never done before. Consider **Figure 6.3**, for example.

Notice, too, that some of the intermediate objectives (prerequisites) are associated with obstacles while others are not. Those "attached" to obstacles have been specifically created to overcome those obstacles. Those without paired obstacles are specific tasks that must be completed, without which the Injection (objective) at the top of the tree can't be achieved. There is no obstacle to their accomplishment — we just can't afford to overlook them.

So, as we look at the Deployment Tree in its entirety, we see a succession of tasks to be accomplished, starting at the bottom and ending at the top. Some are sequential but several can be done in parallel. Some of the tasks are designed to overcome specific obstacles to the overall objective. Others are merely required steps. The output of each completed task becomes the input, or entering argument, for the next one. The last three prerequisites accomplished are the last things that must happen in order to accomplish the objective at the top.

In Figure 6.3, we see the ultimate objective is the accomplishment of an injection for a Solution Tree. It should be clear at this point that some Injections in a Solution Tree can be fairly complicated undertakings. This is why the Deployment Tree becomes a valuable change execution tool.

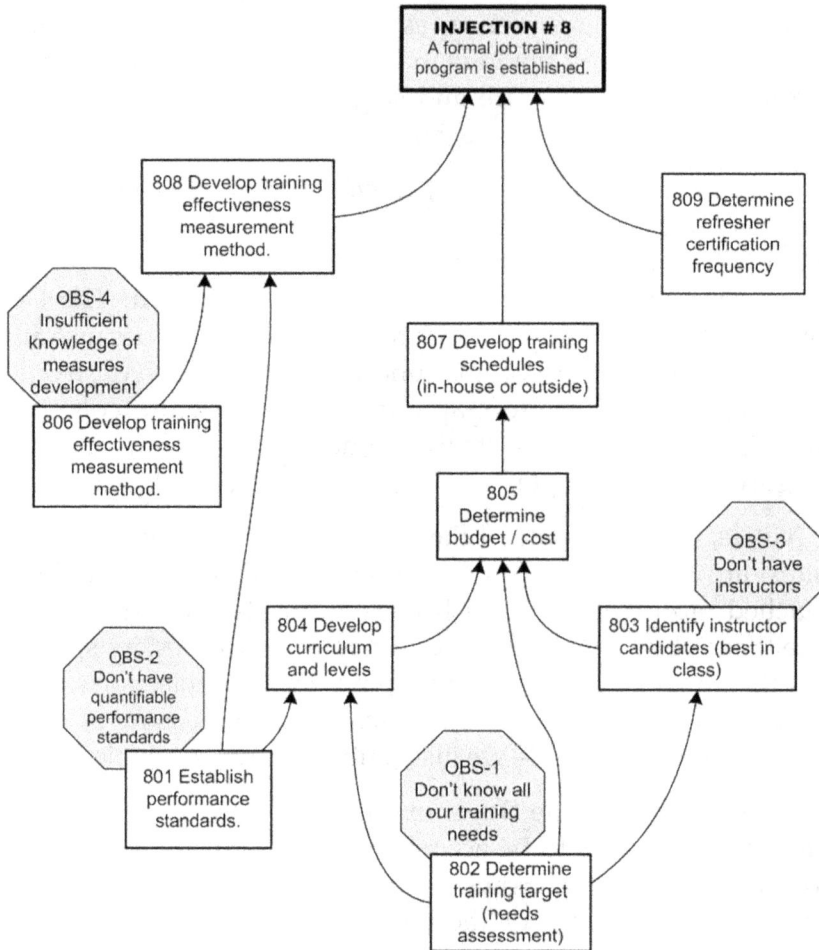

Figure 6.3 – Deployment Tree (job training)

Conclusion

As you can see, the content of the Deployment Tree is very detailed. It's not a broad, system-level tree. In fact, we can consider the Deployment Tree to be a bridge between conceptual solutions and tactical activities. Deployment Trees actually "operationalize" solutions and strategies. Moreover, the detailed nature of this tree suggests that the people best equipped to construct the tree (and the execution plan it embodies) are those who are closest to the work— those who typically live each day with the decisions represented by the Deployment Tree. Consequently, involving those who have an interest in *how* the change is deployed is usually a sound strategy for enlisting their support in making it succeed.

> *The desire to do something good doesn't get it done.*
>
> — *Not attributed* [34]

---

[34] Dettmer. *He Said, She Said*, p.15.

CHAPTER 7.

Putting It All Together

Disorder expands proportionately to the tolerance for it.

— Welwood's Axiom [35]

THE LOGICAL THINKING PROCESS (LTP) represents an orderly way to proceed from an ill-defined problem to a fully implemented solution in complex systems. Founded on deductive logic, it can provide confidence that the problem has been accurately defined and the proposed solution has a high probability of leading to the desired outcome.

In complicated systems, there are very few unitary causes to major problems. A case in point is aircraft accidents. When investigations of such events are complete, the final report may specify a primary cause, but it inevitably attributes one or more contributing (dependent) causes. Just as it's rare for a complicated system's problem to originate from a single cause, so also is it unlikely that one "silver bullet" will be sufficient to cure the situation. Very few problem solving methodologies acknowledge this reality, much less account for it in their execution.

A well-constructed LTP analysis answers four essential questions that all system leaders must understand if they are to succeed:

Why change?

What to change?

What to change *to*?

How to effect the change?

---

[35] Dettmer. *He Said, She Said*, p.114

Why change?

Anytime we examine our system and our situation, we come to one of two conclusions: Everything is okay (no change required) or everything is *not* okay (some kind of change is necessary). We all know that life is not static. The environment changes, we change. So, even if everything is okay now, as surely as the sun rises in the morning, at some point it will not be.

When this happens, we're motivated to change our situation in some way in order to regain that contented equilibrium we recently had. That's the *why*, the motivation to do something differently. But how do we know that everything is not okay in the first place, except through comparison of the status quo with some previously determined standard for what constitutes "okay?"

Consequently, to answer the question "Why change?" we must first clearly define what "okay" looks like and what it takes to make that happen. This is the critical question that must be answered first: *What is our standard for desired system performance?* Hot on the heels of that question is another: *What are the components of system performance that produce that standard?*

Fortunately for us, the Goal Tree provides these answers. And in doing so, it establishes itself as the hub of the Logical Thinking Process Wheel (**Figure 7.1**). It's the immutable benchmark, the channel marker for navigating our way through the process of solving complex problems. Every other step in the process harks back to that essential question the Goal Tree answers: *What are we trying to accomplish?*

What to change?

Once the standard for what *should* be happening is established, and our disaffection with system performance is established, the next question is "What should we change?" What must be different if we're to return our system to the desired state of performance specified in the Goal Tree?

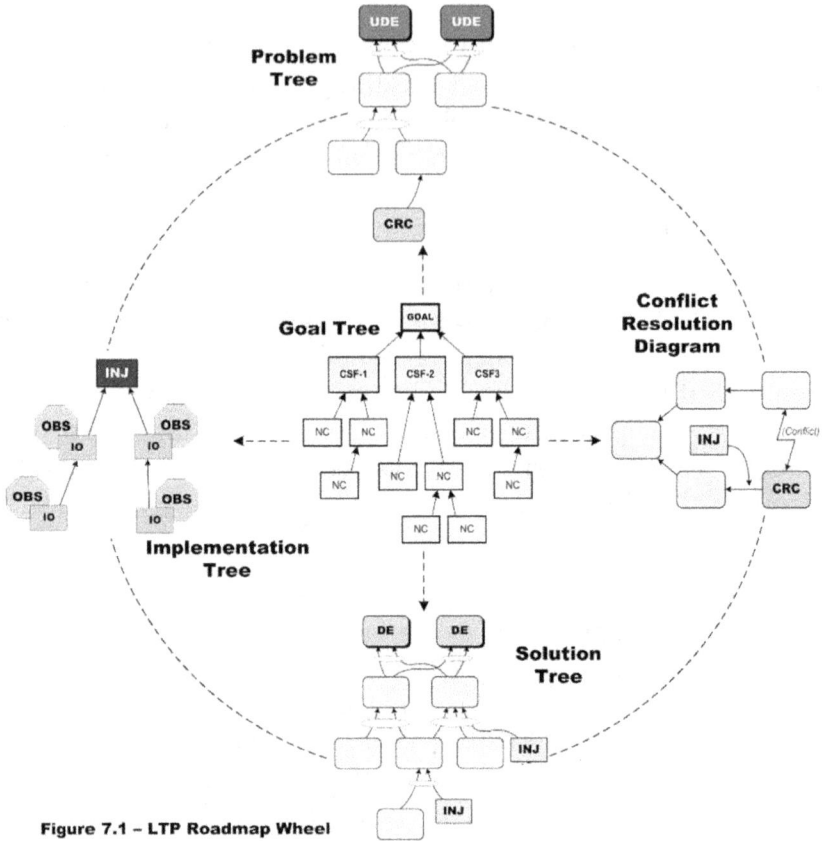

Figure 7.1 – LTP Roadmap Wheel

The answer to this question is provided by the Problem Tree, a logical depiction of current reality that leads us inexorably to the critical root causes producing our disaffection. The Undesirable Effects that reside at the top of the Problem Tree specifically define the gap between what *should* be happening and what actually *is* happening. And the unbroken chain of cause and effect that is the tree itself connects those Undesirable Effects to their indisputable causes.

What to change to?

Once the critical root causes of the system's Undesirable Effects are determined, the obvious next question is what should we do differently? In other words, "What should we change to?"

Answering this question is a two-fold task. First, it requires creativity. Why? Because in many cases—perhaps most—solving the problem will require doing something that hasn't been done before ... maybe even not even contemplated before. Second, changes that have the kind of systemic impact we need for the elimination of Undesirable Effects inevitably disturb—upset, even—somebody's status quo. And for a variety of psychological reasons, people resist having their status quo upset. They don't want to change what they're doing. They're comfortable with it! So, there's an inherent conflict that must be resolved: *change versus don't change*.

Fortunately, this dilemma is easier to address than it might seem with the effective application of the Conflict Resolution Diagram. Besides aiding in resolving the change-don't change conflict, it also stimulates the creativity needed to come up with breakthrough solutions. And the inherent relationship between the Conflict Resolution Diagram and the Goal Tree ensures that whatever new idea is created will actually contribute to— conform to—the ultimate objectives of the system.

However, the job isn't done yet. A creative idea is still only an idea until two things happen: First, it can be proven that the idea will work—that it will actually solve the problem—and that it won't create newer, more contentious problems. And second, it must actually be implemented. In other words, potential energy must be converted into kinetic energy! The LTP provides another critical tool to make the first of these two things happen: the Solution Tree. And once again, the Goal Tree ensures that the proposed solution actually solves the right problems—the system's *critical* problems—because the Goal Tree's critical success factors become the Desired Effects of the Solution Tree.

How to effect the change?

Potential energy is not the same as kinetic energy! The greatest idea in the world is *not* a solution to a problem until it's put into effect—executed! The Implementation Tree is the final step in the LTP. It provides the tactical level detail needed to make the solution work the first time "the key is turned." And it, too, relates to the Goal Tree, because the injection that resides at the top of the Implementation Tree can easily be related to the achievement of one of the Goal Tree's necessary conditions.

Strategy or Problem Solving?

Back in Chapter 2, I suggested that developing system strategy and solving system problems are opposite sides of the same coin. (Figure 2.5) There is more than a little truth to this.

The Goal Tree is at the heart of both, so to continue the analogy we might consider it the coin. The obverse side would be the strategy, and the reverse side would be problem solving. The rest of the logic trees can serve either purpose. Absent an already existing system problem, the LTP can be used to create a strategy for a system when one does not already exist. The completed logic trees, especially the Solution and Implementation Trees, could form the basis of a strategic plan. And, as we've already seen, once such a strategy is established, as entropy raises its head (which it does in all systems), the LTP can be employed to get the system back on course toward the goal established in the strategy.

A Few Examples

With any methodology that has been in use for more than 20 years, as the LTP has, there is no shortage of practical examples of its successful application. In the interest of brevity, I'll describe just three here. Each of them is a complex system, though their sizes differ as do their purposes. Yet each one successfully used the LTP either to resolve complex problems or develop a strategy.

BHP Billiton. BHP Billiton is the merger of two companies, Broken Hill Proprietary of Australia and Billiton PLC of South Africa, to form the largest mining company in the world, with 35 large-scale mines worldwide and annual revenues in excess of $50 billion. Leadership of the resulting entity, BHP Billiton Limited, suffered from significant communication and coordination challenges, owing to the impossibility of integrating two completely different information systems.

In 2008, at the direction of the CEO, BHP Billiton embarked on worldwide effort to install the SAP enterprise resource management (ERP) software to resolve the communication and coordination difficulties and standardize reporting among all of the company's divisions (mines). This was to be a five-year project, culminating in "turning the key" on the new information system in 2013. The problem was that by 2010, it was estimated that going live with SAP was still five years away. The challenge was to resolve what was slowing down the project and to get the SAP implementation back on schedule.

The SAP project team applied the LTP to the problem. Within two weeks, the critical root cause of the inability to progress had been identified in a Problem Tree. A Solution Tree integrated appropriate injections, and Implementation Trees outlined the specific steps and accountabilities to execute the solution. By April 2013, with a lot of hard work by all parties involved, SAP went on line, live, at BHP Billiton—at the originally planned date.

Deloitte and Touche LLC. Deloitte and Touche is one of the largest accounting firms in the world, with $8 billion in annual revenues. It's the accounting arm of Deloitte Touche Tohmatsu Limited, a professional services company that also includes Deloitte Consulting.

Following the collapse of Enron and its accounting firm, Arthur Andersen, in 2001, the US Congress passed the Sarbanes-Oxley Act, which dictated the oversight of accounting firms by an independent board of inspectors. The purpose was to ensure that the large auditing firms—commonly referred to as "the big four"— heretofore unmonitored and unregulated, were never again in the position that Arthur Andersen was of "cooking the books" to satisfy a lucrative client.

As a result of the enforcement of Sarbanes-Oxley, the U.S. Securities and Exchange Commission established the Public Company Accounting and Oversight Board to ensure that the big four auditing firms "minded their P's and Q's." Each year, they inspected, rated, and ranked the four auditing firms. Anything less than a first-place finish in the annual rankings had the potential to cost an auditing firm significant business, as clients defected, taking their auditing needs to the top ranked firm. The first year, Deloitte and Touche LLC finished fourth. Obviously, this was not acceptable to the CEO.

The auditing division brought in Deloitte's management consultants to figure out how to get them out of the basement and up to the top of the heap. Drawing on the expertise of Deloitte's auditing partners, the consultants used the LTP to develop a consensus Goal Tree and a Problem Tree. The Goal Tree established the future strategy for the auditing division, the one that was intended to make them number one among the big four. The Problem Tree identified four critical root causes of their current fourth place standing. The CEO accepted the results of this analysis, saying, "I've been looking for this [the Goal Tree] for 25 years." Over the course of the next two years, the auditing division resolved the critical root causes. Deloitte and Touche LLC is now consistently the highest-ranked auditing company among the big four and the number one, by market share, in the world.

Catalysts GmbH. In 2006, an Austrian IBM software engineer with a Ph.D. in computer programming came to me to learn the Logical Thinking Process. His objective was simple — not easy, but simple. He wanted to use it to design his path to independence. As a salaried software consultant doing SAP installations, he knew that he would always be someone else's employee. But he wanted to build a business of his own. He saw the LTP as his means of creating the strategy to do that.

The tangible result of his LTP training was a complete strategy — the Goal Tree, the Solution Tree, and Implementation Trees that executed it. This strategy laid out his path for the next several years. He returned to Austria and began to work his plan. After a year, he doubled the size of his work force (to two) and occupied a small office along the Danube River. By the end of the second year, he had added four more. In the third year, he added eight contract programmers in Nepal.

By the fifth year, his business had more than doubled — he was up to 20 employees and running out of space in his original small office. In his sixth year, he contracted to occupy the top three floors of a modern office building in the downtown and closed out the year with 95 full time employees — and the contract to develop Volkswagen AG's human resource management software. As of this writing, he has expanded his empire to include offices in the Czech Republic, Hungary, and other central European countries.

It would be wrong to suggest that this success resulted primarily from the strategy he developed using the LTP. Such phenomenal growth needs some opportunities, but mostly it requires exceedingly hard, dedicated work. But his company's nearly exponential growth was certainly facilitated by a robust, logical strategy — which he developed using his innate creativity and the structure provided by the LTP.

Human Factors

Because the LTP is a logical method, its obvious value lies in removing (or at least isolating) the emotional component from decision making — keeping the analysis and problem solving objective. And this has been the emphasis on its use for the past two-plus decades.

However, humans are often anything but logical. In the old "Star Trek" television series, Mr. Spock, the dispassionately logical Vulcan, frequently complained, "Humans are *not* logical." This is largely true, but with an understanding of psychology, human *behavior* becomes eminently logical. In other words, it mostly conforms to well understood psychological principles. And to that extent, it's predictable, *if* we can structure our understanding into a logical framework, such as the LTP.

Here are some of the ways the LTP can be used to understand and deal with the human emotional component in systems in a rational, logical way:

- Resolving interpersonal conflicts

- Understanding why people or organizations behave as they do

- Predicting future behavior

- Anticipating resistance to change

- "Selling" a solution or change to a reluctant audience

There are other uses for the LTP in emotional, political, or social science-type situations. Unfortunately, these are too extensive to go into here. W. Edwards Deming used to say that "the most important figures that one needs for management are unknown or unknowable." [36] He could have been talking about human psychology. Suffice it to say that the LTP is eminently usable for engaging such complex, subjective situations.

Conclusion.

There is much more to the Logical Thinking Process than we've covered here. The LTP is a tool for critical thinking, a skill that is sorely needed (and largely missing) in our society today.

As a tool, however, it's no better than the system knowledge that goes into it. As the old computer idiom "garbage in, garbage out" implies, the quality of your output is dependent on the quality of your input.

Figure 7.2 - The Bullets and the Gun

But there's a better analogy: bullets and a gun. (**Figure 7.2**) Without bullets, a gun is no more useful than a hammer for driving nails into a wall. Add the bullets, however, and its usefulness and power increase exponentially. In the same way, the LTP may well be the ideal systemic logic tool. But without the subject matter knowledge to put into it, it can be an exercise in futility.

The converse, however, is also true. System knowledge without an orderly, logical framework for arranging and evalu-

---

[36] Deming, *Out of the Crisis*, p.121.

ating it is no more than unrealized potential. The Logical Thinking Process can be that framework.

> *Plans get you into things, but you got to work your own way out.*
> — *Will Rogers* [37]

---

[37] Dettmer. *He Said, She Said*, p.101

ACKNOWLEDGMENTS

I WOULD BE REMISS if I failed to acknowledge the people who helped me complete this book you've been reading.

The inspiration for this effort came from Philip Marris, a friendly taskmaster if ever there were one. Christian Hohmann reviewed the manuscript and provided invaluable advice in its improvement.

When my mental well "ran dry," I benefitted from the examples of problems that resulted from bad decision making provided by Romey Ross, Ron Woehr, K.C. Mueller, Bob Elder, Daniel Want, David Hodes, Andy Futey, Paul Selden, Dr. Bert Ray, and Erik Mano.

And finally, the originator of the "thinking processes," Eliyahu M. Goldratt. Though I have modified and refined (and I hope, improved) the logic trees over the past twenty years, they remain the creative brainchild of Eli Goldratt—and, for my money, potentially the greatest of his contributions to the world.

BIBLIOGRAPHY

Deming, W. Edwards. *Out of the Crisis.* Boston, MA: MIT Press, p. 121.

Dettmer, H. William. *He Said, She Said.* San Antonio, TX: Virtual Bookworm, 2013.

Dettmer, H. William, *Strategic Navigation: A Systems Approach to Business Strategy.* Milwaukee, WI: ASQ Quality Press, 2003.

Dettmer, H. William, *The Logical Thinking Process: A Systems Approach to Complex Problem Solving.* Milwaukee, WI: ASQ Quality Press, 2007.

Holley, David. "Toyota Heads Down a New Road," *The Los Angeles Times,* March 16, 1997, BUSINESS, p.D1.

Osinga, Frans P.B., *Science Strategy and War: The Strategic Theory of John Boyd.* New York: Routledge, 2007.

Richards, Chet. *Certain to Win: The Strategy of John Boyd, Applied to Business.* Xlibris, 2004.

www.ingramcontent.com/pod-product-compliance
Lightning Source LLC
Chambersburg PA
CBHW050513210326
41521CB00011B/2447